LA MÈRE BRAZIER

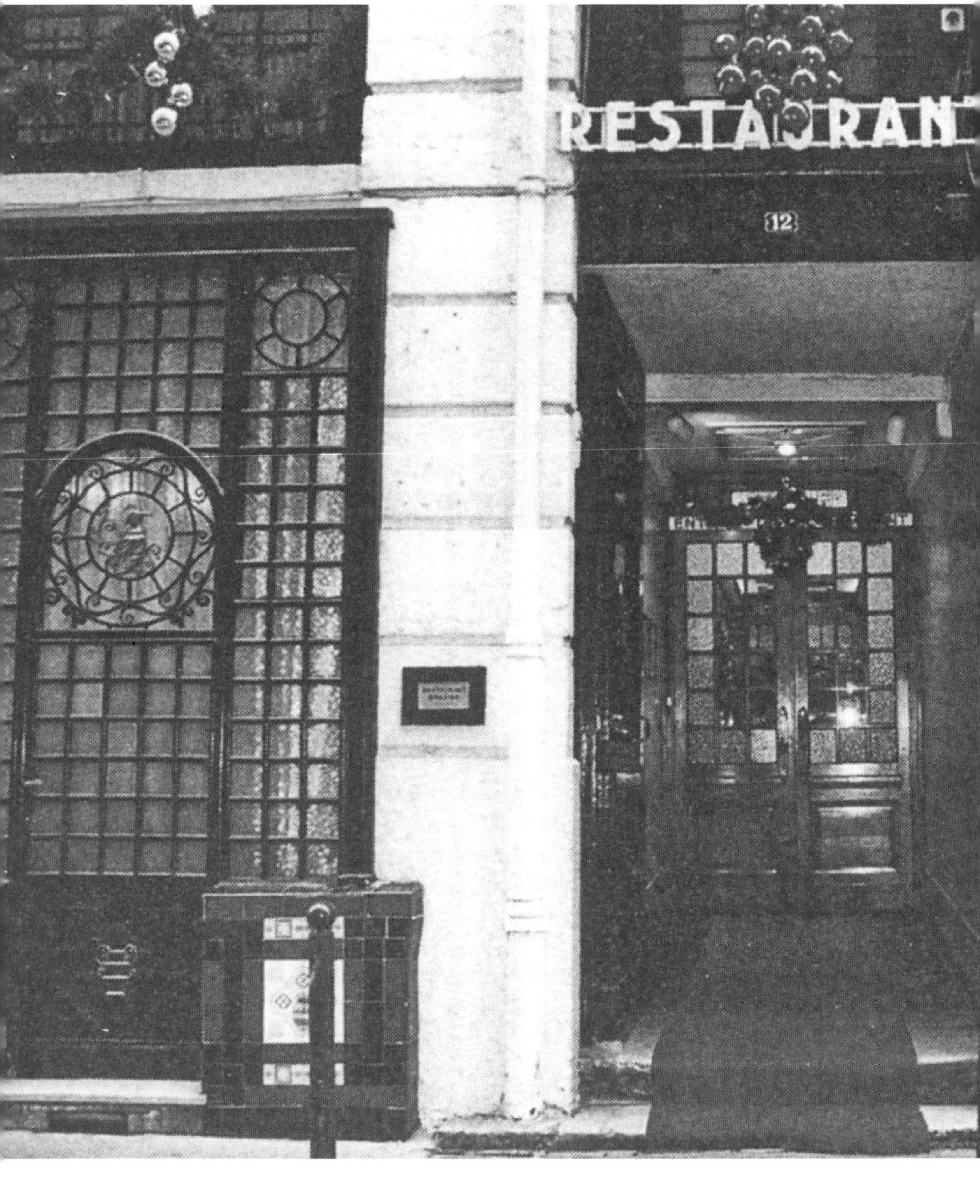
RESTAURAN
12

LA MÈRE BRAZIER

THE MOTHER OF MODERN FRENCH COOKING

EUGÉNIE BRAZIER • FOREWORD BY PAUL BOCUSE

ENGLISH TRANSLATION BY DREW SMITH

RIZZOLI
NEW YORK

New York · Paris · London · Milan

First published in the United States of America in 2014 by
Rizzoli International Publications, Inc.
300 Park Avenue South
New York, NY 10010
www.rizzoliusa.com

English Language Edition copyright: © 2014 Elwin Street Limited
Elwin Street Productions
3 Percy Street
London W1T 1DE
United Kingdom
www.elwinstreet.com

English translation by Drew Smith

Originally published under the title: "Les secrets de la Mère Brazier"
By Roger Moreau, in collaboration with Anne-Marie Brazier, Jacotte Brazier, and
Roger Garnier © 2009 by Éditions Solar, Paris

2014 2015 2016 2017 / 10 9 8 7 6 5 4 3 2 1

ISBN: 978-0-8478-4096-0

Library of Congress Control Number: 2013933348

Photo credits: Éditions Solar: pp. 2, 8, 14, 17, 21, 24–25, 29, 32, 38, 72–73, 80, 89, 94,
103, 122–123, 158-159, 201, 226–227; Bibliothèque municipale de Lyon: pp. 208–209

Illustrations: iStockphoto: pp. 48, 57, 63, 85, 105, 111, 145, 171, 174, 215

Printed in China

CONTENTS

MA MÈRE
BY PAUL BOCUSE

PLENTY OF CHEFS HAVE LEFT A MARK with more or less brio, but few have left such an indelible imprint on the world of cooking as la Mère Brazier, whose legacy—even today—remains one of the pillars of global gastronomy.

This exceptional woman, with whom I had the opportunity to work, taught me some valuable lessons. The only people who counted for her were those who had a taste for hard work; either you stuck by her principles, or you left. It was not a question of having moods or not feeling well or that your shoulder or your hip was hurting, it was required that you were efficient throughout those long, endless days (rising at 5 a.m. going to bed at midnight).

In 1946, I had just been demobilized. I went to present myself for a job as a commis chef. I mounted my bike and climbed up to the col de la Luère, where the famous mother officiated.

I was immediately struck by the intensity of how she looked at me. She was wearing an immaculate white blouse, tied with an equally immaculately clean apron, her hair tied back in a neatly dressed bun, just like the cashier at the Grand Café. When she saw me she said, "A lad who cycles 20 kilometers (12 miles) uphill to come to work must have something about him."

Work was the rule of the house. First to rise, last to sleep, nothing passed her eagle eye. Above all, she wanted everything to be done *à la maison*, even the electricity, which we generated ourselves—no mean feat, that.

So I learned to milk cows, chop wood, garden, do the washing, ironing, look after the wine cellar . . . it was not a case of doing one thing better than another; you had to know how to do everything, and how to do it well.

The era of the thirty-five-hour week had not yet begun, there were no days off to break the rhythm of our weeks and there were not many distractions for young boys like us.

But we invented a game for ourselves on winter evenings, when there were not many customers and when the mother was otherwise occupied with her hard work. We would choose a pig from the pen—each of them handsome, because they were fed on the leftovers from the restaurant—and we would set it free to run wild for miles, with us chasing from behind. Just like the schoolboy apprentice cooks that we were, we had our moments of revolt. We would romp around and we made up a song to the tune of the *La Mer* (The Sea) by Charles Trenet:

| *La Mère qu'on entend gueuler* | We can hear la Mère getting angry |
| *Au col de la Luère* | At the col de la Luère |

But, happily, she knew her own difficult character, and would sometimes ask us to sing the song to her, which made her laugh.

La Mère was a tough and modest woman who knew instinctively how to select the best of us, in the same way that she picked the best produce. The menus hardly ever changed, but were always perfectly executed. The classic standby—the one on which her reputation rested—was Artichokes with Foie Gras (page 56), Quenelles (page 51), Chicken in Half-mourning (with truffles, page 142). The whole world came to eat with us.

Looking back, I can say they were good times, and it is certainly thanks to this woman that my own natural inspiration to create a simple cuisine—not an easy thing—was born. And I owe her, above all, the sense of respect and importance of choosing the right ingredients.

I never forget that I was one of her more remarkable pupils. She taught all of us about flavors and gave us a taste for hard work and work well done. There would have been no success for any of us without her; something we often forget these days.

A PASSION FOR COOKING
BY BERNARD PACAUD

FIFTEEN YEARS AFTER PAUL BOCUSE, I had the same apprenticeship, encountered the same introduction to work, the same conditions, the same admiration of la Mère and, for sure, the same recipes on which the reputation of this exceptional restaurant are based.

In April 1962, I took my bicycle up the col de la Luère. Like many local schoolchildren at Grézieu-la-Varenne, I worked washing-up at La Mère's. After my third shift, she began to encourage me and pointed me toward my future as a cuisinier. It was in this charged, familial atmosphere—albeit very strict and without compromise—that my passion for cooking was born. Every line of this book brings back those memories. Now it is your turn to discover the generous cuisine and spirit of Mère Brazier, in her own words . . .

TRANSLATOR'S NOTE
DREW SMITH

LA MÈRE BRAZIER DIED IN 1977, two years after starting this book. She was acknowledged among many, but most notably by the gastronome Prince Curnonsky, as the greatest cuisinier in the world—in a way, perhaps, of all time. She was the first woman to be awarded three Michelin stars for her restaurant at 12, rue Royale, Lyon. And she was the first chef to be given six stars, in 1933, when her weekend annex 20 kilometers (12 miles) west at col de la Luère, Pollionnay, was also awarded three stars (although at the time, it was nothing but a simple wooden chalet without gas or electricity).

As her fame grew, it was not just the whole of Lyon who came to eat with la Mère, but two presidents of France—Charles de Gaulle and Valéry Giscard d'Estaing were both enthusiasts and advocates. De Gaulle refused to leave and wanted to stay the night, as did film stars like Marlene Dietrich. She turned down offers from the Aga Khan to move to Switzerland, and a potential salary of $150,000 a year to move to the Waldorf Astoria in New York in 1953. A generation of chefs, including Paul Bocuse and Alain Pacaud, learned in her kitchens. It is not going too far to say that her cuisine was the start of modern French gastronomy. The strict regime she applied still informs three-star gastronomy today.

The recipes here are the work of a number of people, principally Roger Garnier, husband of Odette, Eugénie's niece, who was raised as one of her own. Garnier worked for twenty years as chef at col de la Luère. The other recollections were transcribed by Roger Moreau, who taped them from la Mère as she sat on her sofa. They come firsthand to us, as transcriptions of instructions from la Mère herself. It is easy to hear her voice as if she were standing behind you in the kitchen as you prepare a dish.

Garnier and Odette also accompanied la Mère every February on annual note-gathering field trips to France's other great gastronomic restaurants of the time—Point at Vienne, Pic at Valence, Chez Latry at Montélimar, l'Oustau de Thuiller at Les Baux de Provence, la Bonne Auberge at Antibes, and so on . . . re-creating the family pilgrimage south, where she had first learned to cook as a teenage servant.

Always modest, fastidious, moody—perhaps feared for her tempers, which were regular occurrences—and yet revered and loved in the kitchen and by her customers, stories about la Mère are the stuff of legends. When an otherwise upstanding local dignitary begged for discretion having arrived

(Opposite) March 1975: la Mère and Paul Bocuse

with a pretty young companion, she told him, "Monsieur, I understand, just because you follow mass in a cathedral does not mean it is not permitted to say a prayer in a small chapel sometimes." When an architect arrived late for a meeting, she refused to see him until he had been made to clean the windows.

Her chicken supplier quipped that he would soon have to give his cockerels a manicure before bringing them up to her, so fastidious was the inspection of ingredients and their provenance. She was, in fact, markedly faithful to those suppliers over the years who met her exacting standards. She always paid on time, without complaint. But if there was one thing not up to scratch, the whole consignment would be sent back. La Mère rarely went to markets or shops herself, preferring to order after service on the phone—although she expected to be called herself, not the other way round, at 10 p.m. punctual. But she was a tough, shrewd businesswoman, too, paying for her first car, a Peugeot 301, from what she made back from the *triperie*, selling him chicken gizzards.

And she was obsessive about cleanliness, emptying the refrigerators and cold rooms daily so they could be cleaned afresh. Famously, she might patrol the whole house looking for dust. She was also obsessive about waste, overseeing staff dinners herself using the leftovers and the outer leaves of the lettuces, the trimmings from the smoked salmon, or the pancakes. Any food left on a diner's plate went to feed her beloved pigs.

These pigs were raised at the col, and were part of an old custom she carried on throughout her life for a dinner on November 11—St. Martin's Day, traditionally when fall's harvesting is complete. These pigs were killed the night before. La Mère would broil the sausages and blood sausages in a small pan herself, accompanied with small pieces of apple cut into cubes, and pass them around. The main roast was either the whole leg or a side. A big crowd would be invited from Lyon for what was a celebrated feast, also to mark the end of World War II. She would have a band, a clown, and everyone sang "La Marseillaise" through the dinner.

In the translating, I have tried to be faithful to the original idiom. It captures a Gallic way of talking, of doing things, of an era, and a way of life. More than anything la Mère is, and was, a very French icon. Where the grammar is not conventional, it is very instructional. The ingredients appear in the order they are used in each recipe. The home economy of weighing exact measures, we only have in abstract, but just when you read a recipe and something important is about to happen, you will find the necessary clues.

French is a more persuasive and a much more beautiful language than English when talking about cooking. We have "to fry," they have *sauter* or "jump," or *faire revenir*—literally, "bring back to life"—or even *faire respirer*—"let them breathe." We have a poor cliché for whipping egg whites to peaks where la Mère wanted *neige*—"snow," like the snow she could see laying on the Alps from her kitchen window at the col. And salt is not always a noun, but also a verb—that is, do it.

Some recipes, of course, betray their time. The turbot with hollandaise demands a huge oven, but it is many decades, unfortunately, since such fish were landed. The wine recommendations perhaps suffer more than the recipes with the passing of time—exclusively French without vintage or domain. But that was the era. Also, she cooked for more than half a century, in which time such details become obsolete. They remain as pointers and, unlike her other suppliers, la Mère made a point of visiting each of her chosen vineyards.

Other things have been more difficult. *Crème fraîche* has a dual meaning these days, and it is not clear whether the instruction is just for fresh cream or soured, probably the former. Equally *lard*, literally "fat," was different in France from what we find today, so I may have used bacon instead.

The cooking is not in fact elaborate—certainly not by comparison with hotel kitchens of her time—because they did not have the means to produce stocks, fumets, and the kinds of reduction that were the exclusive preserve of grand restaurants and hotels. When Garnier, fresh out of hotel school, produced an elaborate concoction of crayfish as he had been taught, la Mère flew into one of her famous tempers and gave him a proper telling off. ("Of course, she was right and I never forgot the lesson"—the lesson being that a crayfish should be presented simply, steamed, cut in half, and laid on a lettuce leaf.)

The most important thing to la Mère was the freshness of her produce. And the recipes, in fact, revolve around a very limited number of ingredients by modern standards—carrots, onions, shallots, butter—which makes this a very practical, easy-to-use manual.

Some of the recipes are challenging these days, but I have retained them as points of culinary history and, for the most part, anyone with a rudimentary knowledge of the kitchen should be able to master them with a little concentration. Equally I have left in recipes that we take for granted, because la Mère's vinaigrette is not other people's vinaigrette. Nor is her béchamel. Nor are her scrambled eggs . . .

As many others have found, her cooking is a joy.

MY STORY
BY
EUGÉNIE BRAZIER

Roger Moreau, a close friend and
confidant of Eugénie, sat down with
her several times between 1975 and
1976 to talk about her life. This
personal history is extracted from
their many long conversations
from this period.

MY STORY
BY EUGÉNIE BRAZIER

MY PARENTS LIVED AT DOMPIERRE, where my father had inherited a property, a small farm. It was too small to sustain a family, which is why—while I was still a baby—my father decided to take on a bigger farm at Certines on the road to Port-d'Ain à Bourg.

That is where I spent my early days. On this farm, the pigs, the cows, and the horses were my natural companions. Before I was five years old, I was in charge of the pigs. I can hardly remember, but an old servant who stayed with us for many years tells me that is how it was.

Every morning, I had to go out and look after my pigs in the field. If I still remember properly, I recall my mother perching me on a chair each morning to dress me. She would say, "Run quick, run quickly, Augustine has already let the pigs out in the yard!" If I did not jump down quickly enough, I would get a few slaps across the thighs, or at least the promise of them. You can imagine, with such an education, I got into the habit of doing things quickly and not wasting my time! And in my life I don't think I wasted much.

At this time, there was no chocolate in Bresse, and there was no question of us children having tea or coffee with milk. I would leave the house without eating. The field where we kept the pigs was not fenced. The boundary was marked with stones. The pigs had to be kept inside and were not allowed to stray onto our neighbors' land. My role as guardian was important. I was hungry, but I did not dare cry out as I watched the reapers go out to the harvest. I had to wait for their break. Then my mother would bring the soup. I still remember the taste of that soup. It was milky with long slices of bread in it. I have never eaten better!

It was very simple—a broth of leeks and vegetables cooked in milk and water. You whisked in, hard, some egg white and then poured it, bit by bit, onto the yolks in a bowl. You mixed it up well, then poured it over big chunks of bread in a soup bowl and let it soak for a few moments before tucking in.

After feeding the reapers in the field, my mother would come over and sit herself down on a furrow. She made me eat my soup sitting down so that I did not spill it. Even so, you had to eat quickly. Happily the soup had cooled down on its way from the kitchen. Meanwhile, the pigs and Pâquerette, our mare, would wander off to eat the herbs in our neighbors' fields. I had to stop eating and bring them back.

Soup was followed by washing. My mother brought a towel with her, wiped it on the wet clover, and rubbed my nose and cheeks clean. She rubbed

(Opposite) Eugénie Brazier at twenty years of age

hard, because there was no soap, and perhaps this is why I have always had a healthy complexion. The most painful moment arrived with her combing my hair, the comb being yanked down without ceremony. I grimaced without saying anything. She would put my hair up in a bun, tied with a piece of string, which would give her pleasure and make her smile.

And, while all this was going on, Pâquerette was jumping around all playful. I have to tell you about her. She was our mare, but not any old mare. She was a very special horse. She ran at the races. She was a bit of a half-breed. She loved to jump, and to calm her down, we had to put fetters on her. But that would not stop her, the wonderful Pâquerette, especially if a *pétroleuse* came by. The *pétroleuses* were the first cars. They were rare enough. You could hear them coming from a long way off and we would run over to watch them passing. Everyone talked about the De Dion-Bouton cars. And how these Dion-Bouton would drive Pâquerette mad!

She was lithe and had a mean back-kick, as half-breeds often do and this worried my father, especially if he saw me with the little whip I'd made out of string and a nut tree sapling. I enjoyed teasing our mare, but I was always careful about her hind legs and kept my distance and out of the way of her hooves if I gave her a flick of my whip. You see I already had a taste for adventure! Between the *pétroleuses* and me, poor old Pâquerette had plenty to worry about—mostly from me, because the *pétroleuses* did not pass by that often, while I was always there to annoy her.

On the days that we made bread, I was in charge of looking after our mare in the yard and, as you will see, children are often not as naive as people think. At the same time as the bread, my mother would make the tarts. The first was a piece of dough rolled out . . . onto this she would pour a sort of béchamel sauce, into which she had beaten eggs and sugar. We used a large, round, flat wooden spade to lift the tart into the oven.

A second tart was made with onions warmed in the pan with a little butter, salt, and pepper. Then my mother added a bowl of cream. She spread the mix out on the dough and baked it in the oven. Eaten hot, it was pretty good. Aged five, I knew how to cook these two tarts, but I was not allowed to put them in the oven. Alas, because I wanted to. Often, I was not even allowed to touch the dough, it has to be said, because my job was to look after Pâquerette.

If I got bored alone in the courtyard, I would give her a few flicks of my whip to make her jump. My mother would hear the commotion and come and see if I was doing my job properly. If I was being good, then I would get a piece of tart. This trick worked very well many times, and would have continued to do so, had I not been given away by the treason of a farmhand,

(Opposite) Eugénie Brazier with the staff at col de la Luère, her son Gaston to the far right

Émile Lempereur. He loved me well enough. I was his sweetheart and would sit beside him at dinner. But he let the cat out of the bag as far as the horse trick went, and that is my oldest bad memory!

Farms like ours often had children placed with them by the local authorities—we called them little shepherds. We had a girl who was a bit timid and I would tease her a lot. She complained and my father scolded me: "Don't forget, she has red blood in her veins just like you."

And I would get a smack! One day, Émile (him again) advised me not to let such things get me down and it was the kind of advice I kept with me most of my life. So the next day, the two of us—this girl and I—were looking after the cows. She was thirsty. I showed her how to drink from the trough by cupping her hands together, but she would not do it, because she said she was afraid of snakes. So I told her to drink from the buckets of water my mother would fill and bring over for the horses. It was always clean and good to drink, I told her, and went down on my knees to show her how to drink. She was not sure and came forward slowly. Then she leaned forward pursing her lips. That is when I pounced and pushed her head right under the water. I got the biggest ever telling off after that!

I went to school, as and when, only in winter and only when there was no work to do in the house. I was ten when my mother died. I was to be sent out to work, with school reduced to just two months a year. Of course, I was not going to reach any level of education that way.

I was placed with a family on a farm. They did not treat me badly. In the morning we ate soup, pretty much like the one my mother made. At midday we got a piece of bacon fat with cabbage and potatoes. Sometimes we had a gratin of macaroni, cooked first in water, then seasoned with a béchamel of flour, butter, water, and cream. It was the only dish that we ate, but it was good and, much later, my restaurant customers would enjoy it, too.

As employees we were properly nourished (if not quite so well lodged). Friday night was the evening for *gaufres* (somewhere in thickness between a pancake and a waffle). And as I like to put my nose into everything, I got to making the *gaufres*, very simply, with flour, milk, and eggs. We flipped them like pancakes in the pan. With the *gaufres* we were given prunes. It was a party!

I always liked to cook, from way back, and I always liked everything to be clean. If I didn't eat my soup with my mother, my pal Émile—always on my side—would encourage me, but eventually my father got cross and I would blurt out what was worrying me: "I saw Marie make the soup. I am scared. She did not wash the cabbage properly. I don't want to eat it. There might be caterpillars in it." That fear of bugs and caterpillars has stayed with me all my life.

There were always jobs to do on the farm. After looking after the pigs, we had to milk the cows, three times a day, keep up with all the jobs in the house, or gather in the hay . . . without a break, until the evening soup. I say soup, but it was not always soup. In Bresse we often had *gaudes*. It is grilled corn, milled into flour, cooked for a long time in water. I can still see the huge copper pot and the wooden ladles. I can still hear, "Look out, Eugénie, keep stirring that *gaudes* well."

If the *gaudes* was not properly mixed, then it would stick to the bottom and sides of the pan. The youngest children were allowed a little milk with it, but for us, we were always told "You are too big, you are!" Milk had to be kept back to make butter and cheese—precious products, and the surest source of cash for us peasants.

One of the first dishes I knew how to cook is what they call in Lyon a *barboton*. In the big pan used for the *gaudes*, you melt some slices of bacon fat, then you brown onions and garlic, and you put in with them potatoes cut up into thick slices. Then moisten with water and add salt. You let it cook long and slow.

When my parents went to the market fair at Bourg, my mother would bring back some tripe. We waited anxiously to be sure she had not forgotten.

When we killed an animal, we did not throw away the blood. We clotted it and cut it up into pieces and cooked it. It was full of holes. It was not very good, but nothing went to waste.

The "day of the pig" was a big day. I carried on the tradition of making a pork supper on November 11 at my restaurant at the col. The priest at Certines used to come and see me each year right up to his death, and would tell me stories about the local hunt and the dinners he organized for them. He did not like it very much, but it made money for the parish.

ONE OF THE FIRST DISHES I KNEW HOW TO COOK IS WHAT THEY CALL IN LYON A BARBOTON.

How beautiful the women were in their long flowing skirts, veils, and feathers. I can still see them in front of the church, near the cemetery, beside the school. The hunt was always on the day of St. Hubert. What a beautiful spectacle. But it was quickly back to work—quite tough work for a child, but I can say I was never mistreated in any of the places I worked. I had clogs and wool tights; even so, in winter we would get chilblains. I put straw in my clogs to try to keep my feet warm. They were my wages—a pair of clogs and a new dress each year. I liked to clack my clogs and the patron of the house would tell me off for making such a noise. The servants on the other hand encouraged me: "The more clogs you break, the more you earn," they would say. But I would never dare!

When I had been good, the patron would give me her old clothes. I was happy. I did not want for anything. For St. Martin's day I got 40 sous, but they were not for me. I had to give them to my parents.

On Sundays we went to mass. I put on the dress and a hat the patron had given me. It was a beautiful hat. It was made of straw embroidered in blue and white with a big badge that looked like a family of caterpillars (but these were nice caterpillars!). I was very proud of this hat. I fixed it to my bun with a few pins and I felt like a woman!

When my older sister would say, "We were unhappy in those days," I was surprised, because I don't remember being unhappy, except perhaps once, at my first communion. My mother had died and it was my patron who came with me. I was wearing a calico dress from my other sister, who had also died. They had kept the dress and the veil for me that my mother had worn at her wedding. All the mothers made their daughters wear veils. My best friends all knew about my position. They all wore much more beautiful dresses than me. They talked about the presents they had been given: "And your godfather, what did he give you?" "Shoes!"

Me, I had shoes on my feet, and I was very grateful for them. But my friends' mothers did not like them talking about their lovely presents in front of me. For me, I had shoes and the rest did not worry me much.

My patron, in my honor, cooked a big dinner. I remember the dessert—prunes with spoon-shaped biscuits (prunes in wine, if you please). The next day, the priest took us for a walk to Château de Bellevesvre at Dompierre. But the day after, I had to go back to my pigs and my field. It was market day. I was alone and troubled by the thoughts in my head. During the first communion, I could see all the other girls had their mothers with them. I was the only orphan and in my childish mind I imagined my communion was worthless because my mother was not there. I knew my confessions were sincere—that I had followed all the priest's instructions—but without my mother, my communion could never be real. So, in my field, surrounded by all my pigs, I cried and I cried.

A neighbor I knew, Mme. Simonin, came past pushing a wheelbarrow. She saw me crying. She must have thought I had been told off for something. But, when she came back, with her wheelbarrow full, she saw I was still crying, flushed with anger and emotion. She stopped. She cajoled me and asked me questions. Me, I didn't say a word. I didn't dare. Finally, she got

(Opposite) La Mére Brazier's restaurant at the col de la Luère

ENTRÉE
DU
RESTAURANT

cross. She said, "I am going to leave the wheelbarrow here at the entrance to the field. I will take the pigs back to their owners and tomorrow I will take you back to your father, because you are unhappy here!"

Being sent back to your family was seen as a very bad thing, so I told her how I had made a very bad first communion because my mother had not been there. This woman started to cry as much as me. And she told me, "But no. You are wrong. You made the best communion. Your mother was much closer to you than all the others. You remember that." Believe me if you like, but those words have helped me all my life. My two best girlfriends knew unhappiness. One died bringing her second child into the world. I was godmother to her eldest. The other had all sorts of troubles. Me, I have always felt I had better luck than either of them. I am still a believer, even if I do not practice.

In my life I have often regretted not having been to school, but I have always been ready for anything that might challenge me. I have always kept a strict eye on anything done in my name. With the mailman, for example, I won't simply sign for anything. I have always known what I want to say to people to whom I have to write. I make too many mistakes, so I don't write myself, but others have never been allowed to write anything in my name without my checking.

IN MY LIFE I HAVE MET, AND CONVERSED WITH, MANY INTELLECTUALS, SOPHISTICATES, AND I HAVE ALWAYS BEEN MINDFUL OF WHO I AM.

In my life I have met, and conversed with, many intellectuals, sophisticates, and I have always been mindful of who I am. I have an instinct that stops me from putting my feet on ground that is not mine.

Returning to my youth, I was placed on farms until I was twenty. In 1914 I found a job with the family Milliat in Lyon. The Milliats had a bakery in avenue Berthelot. My employer was M. Joseph, one of the brothers. At the time, I had my son and I was not married—something that was definitely frowned upon in those days, especially for a girl looking for a job. Again, I was lucky. My little son stayed with a wet nurse at Dompierre and she needed paying each month.

Joseph Milliat's was a respectable house, fortunately, and they took me in. It was a grand house, well established, but with a big family who needed looking after. All the daughters and the daughters-in-law stayed with us while the men went to war.

I did all the cleaning and all the jobs consigned at this time to the do-it-all help, everything except the cooking. In winter, the family went to Cannes with the servants and help. We lived in a hotel and I looked after the children. Often, to amuse myself, I would tell madam that it was too windy and I could take a cab with the children for a break. It was lovely. We went to Super-Cannes, to the Croix-des-Gardes. There were forests of mimosa in bloom. I had never seen anything like that in Bresse, nor in Lyon. The following summer, the women and children wanted to go to Cannes again and we took a villa.

There, I did everything, including the cooking. I had plenty of mouths to feed. The brothers often came out on leave. But I enjoyed working at the stove and I was happy to let the concierge look after the children. Our old cook had stayed behind in Lyon. She had taught me a little about her craft, but I always put too much water in the chicken with cream to save money. She taught me to swap the water for a few truffles and mushrooms, and I discovered that it was not at all bad.

The *gaufres* we would make at the col, I was already making for the Milliats, just as I had done in Bresse, only the amount of butter changed.

In Cannes I had to go to mass at 5 a.m. each morning and I would do the cooking afterward. I bought fish on my way back from the mass. I remember a bass that surprised me with all its bones. I had cleaned it, laid it in its court bouillon, but then I realized I did not know how to make the hollandaise sauce that had been ordered to go with it.

I did not have any recipe books and I had to ask the concierge for advice. What a secret she shared with me! It was straightforward: no clarified butter or anything complicated like that. In a copper pan, I put eight egg yolks to warm slowly with a little water, without letting it boil, and I added, a piece at a time, two pounds of butter. Nothing more difficult than that. You just have to be careful not to end up with scrambled eggs. If, on other nights, someone wanted a béarnaise sauce, I would sweat down shallots in white wine and then whip in hollandaise, cayenne pepper, and parsley. Cooking is not complicated. You have to be well organized, to remember things, and to have a bit of taste. I learned to cook by doing it, simple as that.

After a few years with the Milliats, I needed to make some more money and I got a job with la Mère Filloux. She had a restaurant on Brotteaux, rue Duquesne, near rue de Créqui. It was a high-class establishment. Père Filloux peeled mushrooms all day while the women looked after the dining room and kitchen. When she got too old, her daughter Mme. Frechin took over the daily routines, while I did the cooking with Mme. Jeanne. It was

(Over) Mère Brazier in front of her restaurant at the col de la Luère, in 1930 23

always women only in the kitchen. But la Mère Filloux was very jealous and was always reprimanding me. I would tell her plainly, "But Madame, that is exactly how you told me how to do it." But she was never satisfied, neither with Jeanne nor me. And I was often reduced to tears. Mme. Frechin always stood up for me, very kindly.

Every Sunday, Madame Filloux would make a rabbit stew for us staff. She always made it herself. The others wanted me to make it. One day la Mère asked the table, "So how is my rabbit stew?" "It is delicious, Madame."

For mine, I used some good bacon from the Auvergne, the very best. One day Mme. Frechin spoke up: "It is good maman, but I prefer Joséphine's!" (Joséphine was me. When I started there was another girl called Eugénie, so they christened me Joséphine instead.) What a drama unfolded! "And why better?" "Because it is darker and I like it better . . ."

I was terrified I was going to lose my job that day. I needed the work. I was looking after my younger brother and my younger sister, and, of course, my little Gaston, who I had now moved up to be with me in Lyon. We rented a place cheaply over a laundromat. I have fond memories of the woman who owned it.

At La Mère Filloux, there were always beautiful chickens, better than you find now. She made a really good dish *volaille demi-deuil* (chicken in half-mourning—that is, the skin stuffed with black truffles, page 142) and she always cooked it very carefully. But her *poulet à la crème* was very simplistic. She would boil up her chicken, throw the cream and mushrooms into a béchamel—just the same way she made a sauce for her *quenelles*—and covered her chicken in it. A quick warm in the oven, and it went to the table. The customers liked it well enough. They were used to it. But I would tell her that her *volaille demi-deuil* was better. "I have never let anyone else handle a chicken in this kitchen except me." So I was the first chef to truss a chicken at La Mère Filloux, but not without a fight. We would wrap them in muslin and then cook them in the stock.

The *menu traditionnel* was:

Fonds d'Artichauts au Foie Gras
Quenelles
Volaille Demi-Deuil
Fromages
Dessert

La Mère Filloux served the artichoke hearts warm, but although I kept this dish on my menus later, I always served the artichokes cold. I find heat spoils foie gras. The *quenelles* were bought in from the Pâtisserie Moine. We only made the sauce, using the mushrooms that old man Filloux kept peeling all day. There were only a few desserts —nearly always ice cream (from Moine again, still in their buckets with their names on them). You can see it was a straightforward cuisine and an easy restaurant to run. In season we would serve a lot of game. It was here that I learned to cook larks, ortolans, and partridges—taken off the bone and chopped and mixed with truffles and foie gras. We often served them with just a salad. Later, I would do a lot less game. It was a famous restaurant, but you had to go through the kitchen to wash your hands and so I would see and meet all the richest people in Lyon of the time . . .

Mme. Filloux was an exceptional businesswoman. She always wore a flannel dress with a small, white crochet necklace. She had a weakness. She would take snuff. I was always worried that her little grains of tobacco would find their ways into my casseroles. I was always a bit of a maniac in that way. At the start of service, she would put on her long flowing dress to greet the customers. We would call this dress the sweeper. It was well named, because it swept up all the sawdust that we would put on the floor in those days.

Mme. Filloux sent latecomers to buy a drink in the neighboring café and we went to get them when their table was ready. She had a talent for recognizing generous clients and avoiding the meaner ones. It is an important lesson in our trade. I got along quite well in this environment, except I always felt that those who could not afford to splash out one day, might be able to another. So I would look after the older ones in particular, because even if they were less well off, they were usually good for telling their friends and passing on advice.

Since we closed the restaurant in August (for the annual holidays), I went back to the Milliats. Then, the next year to the Brasserie du Dragon in rue de la République. There were not many gastronomic restaurants in Lyon in those days—La Mère Filloux, La Mère Buisson in rue du Garet, and a few others whose names I forget. The Brasserie du Dragon was very well known, and even though I had only signed on for a month, I stayed on through September because I was better paid, and a few more years after that . . . It was a very agreeable house with clientele who liked me and my son. The cuisine was simple, and yet wholesome, which immediately created confusion. As I was doing the cooking at the Dragon, many customers thought this was Mme. Filloux's new restaurant. When they told me this I would say, "No," and send them back to the rue Duquesne, but one day one of the clients told la Mère,

"We ate a marvelous roast chicken with a superb jus at the Dragon, and delicious green beans . . ."

Mère Filloux answered, "But she—she, was my—she never cooked here. She was just a washer-up." See how jealous she was!

The customer replied, "So it is even better, all the more credit to her!"

Usually the girls always helped me, like Jeanne the *cuisinière*, my colleague, and even when I was in prison during the war they would say, "It is not possible, she who brings so many people to Lyon."

Père Visseau told them, "There has to be a head Turk in each profession," and I suppose that hat fitted me.

After a few years at the Dragon, I wanted to set myself up in my own business. One day, when I was going to pick up my *quenelles* from the pâtisserie by my apartment, the baker told me, "If you want to set yourself up in your own place, there is a grocery-cum-bar round the corner that might suit you." But I am no barman. I have no time for drinkers who sit around chatting all day long. So I bought the shop and straightaway I took the bar out. Above the grocer's I also inherited some lodgers. At the Dragon I had a few regulars who used to like me, because they would sometimes turn up quite late when I was getting ready to leave and the brasserie was closing: "Ah what a pity, you are leaving. We are hungry, but you already have your hat on to go," they would say. "But my hat is not stuck on . . ." I would take it off and give them something to eat . . .

I only had 12,000 francs in the bank. I had put 2,000 down as a deposit, but I hardly had enough to buy ingredients or wine, which is where the owner of the Dragon helped me out. Something else helped, too. The landlord let me settle month to month. We moved in, a bit at a time, with what we had. I was not officially married, but everyone knew my partner. He worked as a chauffeur with a family on quai Gailleton. When he got back at night, he swept the dining rooms, sharpened the knives, and prepared the wine carafes. Me, I did the washing. Always white linen, of course.

I remember my first menu. It was a Sunday that stays in my mind like one of the great worries of my life. I knew Mme. Masson, supplier to the Dragon, who gave me some useful advice. She encouraged me to put crayfish on the menu, which I could take back to her if they were not sold by four in the morning . . . So I planned my menu as small crayfish with mayonnaise, pigeons with peas (which, because I had nearly twenty lodgers would always get eaten the next day). I worked out that while the crayfish were being served, I had time to roast the pigeons.

(Opposite) A portrait of Mère Filloux

But that Sunday at midday—no one showed. At 1 p.m., still nobody. My son Gaston said to me, "You see, Mom, I think you made a mistake buying a restaurant. We should have bought a haberdashery." He had become friends with a neighbor who ran a haberdashery and would fix his buttons when I did not have time. He would take her some soup and the two of them would gossip. He had noticed that she got a lot of orders and that made an impression on him, but he did not understand that each of those orders was only worth 20 sous.

All afternoon, I was desperate, but that evening the restaurant was full. I had fifteen customers. For dessert, I did not want to buy anything that might spoil. We did not have any refrigerators back then. My other neighbor, the baker, had lent me some brioches, which, like the crayfish, I could return in the middle of the night if they had not sold. It was a time when we all made do. Gaston loved apples baked in a pan and flambéed in rum. Later on, he would always serve it to his own restaurant customers. I followed his idea. I hollowed out the brioches and filled them with baked, flambéed apple, served hot. Everyone was happy. This menu was worth 5 francs.

I NEVER HAD THE TIME TO RUN AROUND. I PHONED MY SUPPLIERS, WHO TOLD ME WHAT HAD COME IN AND WHAT WAS GOOD, AND THEY WOULD DELIVER.

All that passed in April, 1922, but when winter came, I had no heating except a stove that had to glow completely red to heat the dining room. It was dangerous. In those days, my days were pretty full. I was up at 7 a.m. to iron the tablecloths, which were still damp from washing after dinner the night before. Sometimes I would even have to put them back on the table not quite dry. After the ironing, the two girls who worked the dining room would arrive and set the tables. My partner, these two girls, an old woman, and me—that was the entire team.

For shopping, I never had the time to run around. I phoned my suppliers, who told me what had come in and what was good, and they would deliver. I changed my menus a little according to the seasons: one day it might be pike, another it was perch or a blood sausage, with fries. A gratin of macaroni (page 77) was reserved for days when there were not many vegetables about.

There were quite a few accidents . . . One day, when I was making spinach, a beautiful woman walked past the kitchen and a flick of green juice caught the white brim of her hat. I can still see it, that damned stain, but she never saw it, or if she did later, she never guessed it was spinach juice. Old Marie who worked with me said, "Don't worry, she will think it was one of the pigeons on the roof!"

We got away with that one, but another time Marie had a similar mishap with a customer who ate with us every day. He was the salesman for Say sugars, M. Chemot—an elegant Lyonnais businessman, who wore a coat with a blue velvet collar and always clean white gloves. But this day Marie took his coat and as she was passing the kitchen caught a little butter on the collar by mistake. Knowing how fastidious this gentleman was, I was horrified. We tried to clean it, but nothing worked. So I ran quickly to the cleaners who managed to get rid of the stain, but there was still the smell. Marie poured some ammonia on the stain to get rid of the smell, or so she thought, but it made matters worse. The moment arrived where we had to give this gentleman back his overcoat. An explanation was needed: "Excuse us M. Chemol, your coat was next to that of a woman who was wearing so much perfume that it has rubbed onto your coat."

"Oh, these woman have strange habits," he said. I learned how to tell a few untruths, as you see.

You could only reach the wine cellar from outside. My partner, who had more imagination than me, managed to make a hole in the floor that let you drop things down without having to go outside. He arranged a dessert table over the hole, which was very useful.

On our own, bit by bit, we managed to open a second dining room. Then, when I managed to find us somewhere else to live, we made two more dining rooms on the first floor. The problem was always chairs. At the start, when my neighbor, the baker, saw a group arriving with us, she would tell her daughter, "Quick take some extra chairs round to Mme. Brazier. Run quickly." When I had enough money, I bought two chairs, then later I could afford to buy four at a time. The seller asked me one day: "Why are you buying chairs two at a time? How many do you need?" "I don't know, twenty maybe forty . . ."

One or two days later, I was rinsing out my washing in the street by the fountain at the junction of rue Royale and rue Marceau, to save water. I heard a lorry stopping. I went to see and saw a consignment of chairs. Lucky for some, I thought. But then I realized the lorry was outside the restaurant and a woman was getting out. "We are bringing you some chairs."

"You are mistaken, I did not order any."

"No, you didn't order any, but I know your customers sometimes do not know where to sit. I don't like them standing up. I am not asking you for any money. Pay me when you can."

And she ordered the driver to take the chairs in. This woman was Mme. Bonjour, of cours de la Liberté. Every month I would cross over the Morand bridge to take her 10 or 20 francs. This debt worried me, because I was not making that much money with my menus at five francs. But I managed to pay her back soon enough.

Doctors were among my first customers and they told everyone about us. There was one customer in particular that everyone knew, President Herriot. He had eaten at the Carillon, with Vettard, but he used to come more and more often to eat with me. He would often arrive early, sit down on the steps, and get in the way of the service—but in a charming way. You could have said he was a big eater. He liked simple, good food—a warm sausage, chicken in a cream sauce. Me, I did not have any caviar or smoked salmon at that time, but that did not worry him. Césarine was his secretary. She came, each evening, looking for something for the president to eat, because he worked very late. Sometimes I would make foie gras for him, even if it was a bit too fattening for his diet. Césarine would smuggle it secretly to him, out of sight of Mme. Herriot.

Later, when he gave a grand reception in Paris at Vettard, he demanded my son Gaston should be there to help. The *Président* commanded! I remember, after he died, a conversation at the col, in which some gentlemen were criticizing Herriot. One of them stood up and said something that pleased me: "Yes, but if he walked in now, you would all stand up and shake his hand." He was an honest man. I have not met anyone more so. He would often annoy me in the war years, when there was rationing and he would bring me plenty of customers, but it was strictly prohibited to have bills of more than 200 francs. You had to pay crazy prices at the time, I never made a profit. But he did not care. He was not rich and money did not interest him. But to eat well was important to him and this often embarrassed me. But he also did me some great favors.

One day there was to be a big dinner at a hotel at Lugdunum for the local hunt. I was asked about the menu and suggested some simple dishes, but added, "But if you are eating at Lugdunum, you had do better to ask the cooks there to cook some classic dishes that you enjoy."

"But we want it to be your cuisine."

"Then come up to the forest at the col de la Luère and eat in the open air like real hunters."

(Opposite) The restaurant staff at the dedication of la rue Eugénie Brazier

A few days later they came to see me. "OK, we will come and eat with you, but we want our patron (Herriot) to be there, and he won't travel that far."

"I bet he will come."

"OK, if he comes, we will pay for the dinner. If he does not come, then we won't pay."

"Agreed."

I was a bit worried, because there were more than one hundred guests. I told Césarine. She rang me back: "The boss is in a good mood, come and see him, he will be up soon."

I smartened up quickly and put some rice powder on my nose and set off. He lived at Herbouville, quite close to me. He heard me coming in. "It is you, la Mère. Come in."

I saw him, a big man in his pajamas, unshaven, but smiling. "So my beauty [his words], Césarine told me the story. Don't worry! I will be there."

What a relief! But it did not last, because on the day of the banquet Césarine phoned me to say the president had had an attack of colic. He could not come. But he came anyway, with his Russian hat, and tunic undone. He was not well enough to attend the banquet. He ate with me in the kitchen, and with Henri, his chauffeur. He left quietly. But he came and I was paid. I can still see him, walking painfully back to his car, in his old tunic of which Césarine remarked, "The whole world offers you statues, paintings, and biographies, could they not at least find you a new tunic?"

Speaking of Herriot, I skipped a few years. What really made me well known, after the doctors, was Spidoleine, which was an oil for cars. This company organized a big car rally across Europe. One year, they came to Saint-Fons in the suburbs of Lyon. The director was M. Serge André. He came to eat at rue Royale and he asked me to prepare a cold picnic for the drivers, mechanics, and organizers. Since he liked what he found in his picnic basket, M. André asked me to go up to Paris every year to cook the Spido banquet. I had to take everything—the chickens, the *quenelles*, all the ingredients. I was not used to cooking for Parisians and I could have made a few mistakes. So I also took a few Lyonnais who were used to working with me. There were more than two hundred covers. This success in Paris brought yet more customers to the rue Royale, and during the Lyon festival, it was crazy. There were so many people I put tables on the sidewalk . . .

All this exhausted me and I had to have a rest, leaving the business to my son, Gaston, to look after. I knew he could keep up the standards and the level of cooking by then. I was then offered some land with an old wooden building at the col de la Luère. But there was no water, no gas, no electricity. It was a resting place, pure and simple. But, as I started to feel better, I began to do a few *casse-croûtes* for my old customers when they came to see me and slowly, step by step, I built up a second restaurant. But everything had to be built. I wanted the customers who thought it worth traveling up into the hills, and 20 kilometers (12 miles) from Lyon, to find all the comforts of a proper house. That was the ambition, simply put, of my establishment.

During the war there was rationing, and I had a few troubles. You know that my cooking is not made with any old thing and I often did not stick strictly to the rules. I was given some hefty fines over and again, the restaurant closed, and I even spent a week in prison. When we reopened the restaurant at the col, all my old clients came back.

One day, at rue Royale a large family party arrived, followed by a gentleman dressed in a gray uniform. At this time well-to-do families often still had a chauffeur. I took this man to be the chauffeur, especially when he said to me, "Excuse me, Madame, would it be possible for me to eat something?"

I was angry at the family neglecting their employee, so I invited the man into the kitchen, and while everyone else was busy I looked after him myself. I always had a few places set for those in service. A few minutes before, a customer had given me some noodles to cook for her dog—beautiful white noodles, the kind you hardly see these days. I gave the dog's noodles to my chauffeur and some gray and dirty leftovers to the woman's dog. With a little jus poured over, the dog did not notice and nor did his owner. With the noodles, I served my chauffeur a piece of *entrecôte*. I even added some butter and told him to eat it out of the pan because I did not have any hot plates in the kitchen. When he left, the "chauffeur" said, "Thank you, Madame, I have eaten wonderfully well. I am just back from a tour of duty of the Midi, where I saw wonderful flowers, but nothing of interest on the plates. Tonight, for dinner, I will tell the field marshal that I have eaten the best noodles of my life. For sure, he will say to me, 'Yes, you look well fed, you must have stopped at La Mère à Lyon . . .'" My chauffeur was General X. [La Mère refused to give his name.]

Me, I never play politics. I cook the best possible, that is all. The big loss I have had was to lose my son, Gaston. But that house has been maintained by my daughter-in-law and my little girls who keep up the tradition . . .

As told to Roger Moreau, 1975–1976

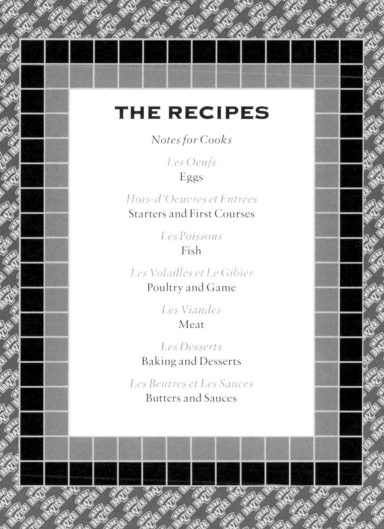

THE RECIPES

MÈRE BRAZIER

12

ENTRÉE DU RESTAURANT

NOTES FOR COOKS

This book comes from an oral tradition of cooking—many of the recipes were transcribed from interviews and were never written down. Though the recipes in this book are very practical, some elements may be different from what we are used to now. In order to preserve la Mère's style of cooking, we have decided to treat these recipes as historical documents and not change them in any way.

Obviously la Mère would have butchered her own chickens and cleaned her own fish, and so, out of interest, we have left her notes from the original translation. We suggest that you have your local butcher or fishmonger prepare the mentioned cuts of meat or fish for you. They may also be able to suggest appropriate substitutes should you not be able to find a particular kind of meat or cut in your area.

INGREDIENTS are listed in order of importance or usage.

QUANTITIES are only precise where they have to be; otherwise you need, for instance, enough stuffing for the size of your chicken or enough vegetables to fit into your pot.

STEPS for each recipe are in a strict order to follow.

OVEN TEMPERATURES in the restaurant would have been top shelf, middle shelf, or bottom shelf and, therefore, are not ultraprecise. They translate as:

Gentle or low:	190 to 250 °F
Medium:	320 to 400 °F
Hot:	410 to 465 °F
Very hot:	520 to 570 °F

COOKING TIMES are no different than the cooking times today; however, because these dishes were originally meant to be served in a restaurant, there are instructions to serve all dishes on very hot plates and then take them straight from the kitchen to the table without delay.

SAUCES have their own section at the back of the book but one technique, *Beurre Manié* (see page 254), is used throughout to bind the sauces and is worth keeping in mind from the start.

(Opposite) The entrance to Mère Brazier's restaurant today in rue Royale, Lyon

LES OEUFS
EGGS

OEUFS BROUILLÉS

SCRAMBLED EGGS

This is, perhaps, the finest method of cooking eggs. It is important to take a few precautions to achieve the right degree of cooking so that the dish is creamy, mellow, and soft.

BUTTER
EGGS
SALT
PEPPER
HEAVY CREAM
(OPTIONAL)

Lightly melt a nut of butter in an ovenproof, porcelain casserole or cast-iron dish. Pour in the beaten eggs just as for an omelet; salt and pepper. Let them cook over a very low flame or—better—in a bain-marie, until they are smooth. Let them cook, stirring all the time with a wooden spoon.

As the mass starts to take hold, turn off the heat. Add extra ingredients as you like.

At the last minute you can add a few nuts of butter or heavy cream. Serve in small porcelain molds or on small warm plates.

OEUFS SUR LE PLAT

EGGS ON A PLATE

Preparing oeufs sur le plat *is an art. Fernand Point, the celebrated cuisinier at la Pyramide in Vienne, judged the quality of his students by how they cooked this dish. La Mère used a very large saucepan and, holding it an angle, she slipped the hot butter onto the yolks. Serve with country bread.*

BUTTER
EGGS
SALT
PEPPER

Put a porcelain pan over a flame. Allow a piece of butter just to melt in it. Break the egg onto a plate and slide it into the pan. Cook over a very low flame so the white becomes milky and the yolk has time enough to warm.

To the side, melt another piece of butter, salt and pepper it, and at the last moment, pour onto the egg yolks.

OEUFS À LA CANTALIENNE

EGGS WITH CANTAL CHEESE

This dish also works with Gruyère cheese.

EGGS
SALT
PEPPER
BUTTER
HEAVY CREAM
CANTAL CHEESE

Take 2 eggs for each guest. Separate the whites from the yolks. Whisk the whites until they are very firm and, at the last moment, salt and pepper lightly.

Butter a deep, round gratin dish. Spread the egg-white mix in a layer and make a hollow for the yolks. Pour the yolks into the hollows, pour over a teaspoon of cream. Scatter on top slices of Cantal. Place in a warm oven for 10 minutes.

OEUFS POCHÉS

POACHED EGGS

Eggs cooked like this serve either as a garnish or to accompany vegetables.

EGGS
SALT
VINEGAR

Bring a saucepan of water to a boil with 2 teaspoons of salt and a spoon of vinegar per quart.

Break the eggs close to the boiling water and allow to fall in carefully. Leave to poach for 3 minutes without letting the water boil again. The whites should be just thick enough to imprison the yolks, which ought still to be liquid.

Lift the eggs out with a slotted spoon, refresh in cold water, and drain on a napkin.

For deviled eggs, poach and put back into the warm (empty) pan—carefully, so as not to break them. Then slide them onto a hot plate. Put a nut of butter in the pan to warm, until it turns nutty . . . add a splash of vinegar and pour both onto the eggs.

OEUFS FRITS

DEEP-FRIED EGGS

Deep-fried eggs are less familiar in France. These eggs are generally used as a garnish, either for chicken or for vegetables.

EGGS
OIL TO COVER EGGS
SALT
PEPPER

To fry the eggs, warm the oil—preferably in a small pan, because it is only possible to do one egg at a time. When the oil is very hot, slide in an egg that you have broken onto a plate, seasoned with salt and pepper. Stir strongly with a wooden spoon, so that the white completely encloses the yolk.

Drain the egg on a napkin and start the operation again for the next egg.

OEUFS EN GELÉE

JELLIED EGGS

ASPIC JELLY
   (PAGE 266)
TRUFFLE
PUREE OF GOOSE
   OR DUCK LIVER
OEUFS POCHÉS
   (PAGE 43)
BAYONNE HAM

Pour a little good-quality gelatin into small molds. Let it set and lay on a slice of truffle, a layer of liver puree, a poached egg, and a julienne of Bayonne ham. Fill up with gelatin. Leave to cool and set.

Unmold and serve very fresh.

OEUFS EN COCOTTE

EGGS IN A COCOTTE

BUTTER
EGGS
HEAVY CREAM
   (OPTIONAL)
HERBS (OPTIONAL)
SALT
PEPPER

Warm some small, ovenproof, porcelain cocotte dishes in the oven with a nut of butter. Take out and place in a bain-marie. Break the eggs—in principle 2 per cocotte—and cook in the bain-marie over a flame for about 10 minutes. The length of cooking depends on the thickness and size of the dish.

You can add, just before serving at the end of the cooking, a teaspoon of very fresh cream and a few fresh, chopped herbs to each cocotte. Salt and pepper lightly.

OEUFS AU VIN ROUGE DE SANCERRE

EGGS IN RED WINE

2 EGGS PER PERSON
SALT
PEPPER
5 OR 6 SMALL
   ONIONS
1 CUP RED SANCERRE
BEURRE MANIÉ
   (PAGE 254)

Put in a casserole 2 cups of salted and peppered water. Finely chop 5 or 6 onions and add to the water. Leave to bubble quietly for 10 minutes. Drain, add the red wine, and cook for another 10 minutes.

Poach the eggs in the liquor for 10 minutes so they are hard, and keep warm.

Bind the sauce with the *beurre manié* to get a smooth, but not too thick, sauce. Pour the sauce over the eggs and serve very hot.

SYMPHONIE D'OEUFS

SYMPHONY OF EGGS

14 EGGS
SALT
PEPPER
SAUCE TOMATE
   (OPTIONAL)

Eggs should not be hard-boiled more than ten minutes.

Hard-boil 2 eggs and chop them finely.

Poach 4 eggs and keep them warm.

Make 4 small omelets of 2 eggs each, very thin. Spread them with the chopped hard-boiled egg and place a poached egg in the center. Fold over the sides and slide onto a hot plate.

Serve with these little omelets a good *Sauce Tomate* (page 264)—very hot.

OMELETTES

OMELETS

Omelets are quick and easy to make and can accommodate many flavors. In general we recommend adding to well-beaten eggs seasoned with salt and pepper, one or two spoons of heavy cream. It lends smoothness to an omelet. The success of an omelet depends on different factors, such as the pan itself—the bottom should be completely flat—and an even spread of butter. At the same time it is better to warm the pan before you start cooking and always have a good flame going. To make a classic omelet, heat some butter in a flat pan. Once the pan is hot, pour on the egg mixture. Fold the omelet over as it sets.

MOUSSELINE: Mix the egg yolks with an equal measure of heavy cream, whisk the whites to a firm snow, and fold back into the yolks. Pour into a warm pan with a good piece of butter. Fry the omelet, flicking the edges back into the center. Turn over and sauce as a plain omelet.

ESPAGNOLE: Add chopped onions sweated in butter, some *Sauce Tomate* (page 264), and chopped parsley.

AUX FINES HERBES: Add finely chop parsley, chervil, tarragon, and chives. (Or sorrel sweated in butter.)

FLORENTINE: Add spinach cooked down in butter.

LORRAINE: Broil some bacon lardons and slip onto the omelet with slices of Gruyère cheese and chopped chives.

PARMENTIER: Sauté some potatoes cut into tiny cubes. At the end of the cooking add in the eggs and leave to cook flat.

SAVOYARDE: Add to the egg mix some thinly sliced sautéed potatoes and slices of Gruyère cheese. Leave the omelet to cook flat.

VOSGIENNE: Add to the omelet some smoked ham and Gruyère cheese.

OMELETTE CHASSEUR

HUNTER'S OMELET

EGGS
CHICKEN LIVERS
MUSHROOMS
SAUCE TOMATE
  (PAGE 264)
PARSLEY
SALT
PEPPER

Finely chop some chicken livers and warm through with some chopped mushrooms. Hold back 2 spoonfuls of this mix and give the rest a little *sauce tomate*. Keep warm without letting it boil.

Make a classic omelet and, before folding it over, spread the sauce over the top. Turn and place on a hot plate. Make a slit down the middle and fill with the reserved mushrooms and chicken livers. Sprinkle with chopped parsley.

Serve on very hot plates.

This can also be made with kidneys: Slice veal or lamb's kidneys into dice and cook in butter. Make the omelet, split in half lengthwise, fill with the kidneys, and surround with a little *sauce tomate*.

Other fillings might include sweated mushrooms, truffles, shelled shrimp, croutons, etc.

OMELETTE RICHEMONDE

RICH MAN'S OMELET

MUSHROOMS
BUTTER
EGGS
HEAVY CREAM
SAUCE HOLLANDAISE
  (PAGE 257)
SALT
PEPPER

Carefully wipe the mushrooms clean, slice, and sweat in butter. Add 2 or 3 spoons of fresh cream, depending on the importance of the omelet.

Make an omelet and fold over in the pan.

Lay it up on a hot plate. Split it lengthwise and fill with the sauce of mushrooms. Cover with the hollandaise and serve straightaway.

GÂTEAU DE FOIES DE VOLAILLE

A CAKE OF CHICKEN LIVERS

Careful! As with a soufflé, this dish must not wait once it is ready. It must be served immediately. The sauce tomate, *the cockscomb, and the chicken kidney need to be stewed ahead with the mushrooms.*

CHICKEN LIVERS
PARSLEY
CHERVIL
SAUCE BÉCHAMEL
   (PAGE 255)
4 EGGS, SEPARATED
SALT
PEPPER
BUTTER
BREAD CRUMBS
SAUCE TOMATE
   (PAGE 264)
1 COCKSCOMB
1 CHICKEN KIDNEY
FIELD MUSHROOMS
GREEN OLIVES

Trim the livers neatly of any sinew and leave them to soak and cleanse in fresh water. Drain, wipe dry, and chop with a handful of washed and dried parsley and chervil.

Make a thick béchamel with a good measure of butter and flour using 2 cups of milk. Leave to cook for a few minutes.

Off the stove, use a wooden spoon to incorporate 4 egg yolks. Add in the chopped liver hash, salt, and pepper. Whip the egg whites until they are a firm snow, and fold into the mixture carefully, as for all soufflés.

Butter a round mold, sprinkle with bread crumbs, and half-fill with the mixture. Cook in a bain-marie in a medium oven for about 20 minutes. The cooking must start very gently.

Turn out into a large bowl and surround with a good *sauce tomate*, adorned with field mushrooms, the cockscomb, the kidney, and green olives.

SOUFFLÉ DE JAMBON CUIT

HAM SOUFFLÉ

To be sure the soufflé does not stick to the sides of the mold, powder it with flour before pouring the mix in.

Proceed as for the Gâteau de Foies de Volaille *(opposite), but replace the chicken livers with one pound of lean ham, chopped in a grinder. You can also add some grated Parmesan cheese into the béchamel.*

ALEXANDRA: Add into the ham soufflé some asparagus tips, cooked and sautéed in butter. Finish with a layer of truffles.

PÉRIGOURDINE: In the mold, alternate a layer of soufflé mix with a layer of thinly sliced truffle. At the moment of service, sprinkle over some chopped truffle.

CARMEN: Put in the ham soufflé dish 2 or 3 layers of tomatoes melted in butter and a sweet pepper.

♀ Pouilly-Fumé, white Hermitage, Alsace

SOUFFLÉ AU FROMAGE

CHEESE SOUFFLÉ

4 TABLESPOONS
BUTTER
½ CUP FLOUR
1 CUP MILK
SALT
PEPPER
NUTMEG
1 ¼ CUPS GRATED
GRUYÈRE CHEESE
4 EGGS

Melt the butter in a thick-bottomed casserole. Mix in the flour and moisten with the boiling milk. Salt, pepper, and grate a little nutmeg. The sauce should have the consistency of a thick béchamel.

Off the fire, add a nut of butter and incorporate the egg yolks, one by one, working well with a wooden spoon. Add 1 ¼ cups of grated Gruyère. Beat the 4 egg whites to firm peaks and fold into the sauce.

Pour into a buttered soufflé dish. Only fill the dish halfway. Sprinkle with grated Gruyère. Bake in a medium oven for 30 to 40 minutes. Serve in its mold.

♀ White Mâcon, Pouilly-Fumé

SOUFFLÉ AU SAUMON

SALMON SOUFFLÉ

This dish is like a quenelle, *but is easier to achieve if you have not got all the equipment of a professional kitchen. This recipe is for 15 portions, because it can be kept frozen perfectly well for two or three months. The recipe can be made using any fish.*

1 LB SALMON
2½ CUPS BUTTER
10 EGGS
2 TEASPOONS PEPPER
2 TEASPOONS SALT
2 CUPS HEAVY CREAM
OIL

Put the fish in a mixer to reduce it to a puree. Add the butter and keep mixing. Add to the mix—one at a time—the eggs and the seasoning. Add in the cream and keep beating to get a smooth mousse.

Put the mixture into ovenproof glasses, goblets, or teacups so they are three-quarters full. Don't forget to grease the insides of the glasses or cups with oil so they are easier to unmold at the end. Cook for 30 minutes in a bain-marie in a medium oven.

You can serve these soufflés straightaway or keep them in the freezer.

To serve: In a gratin dish, melt a nut of butter in some salted water. Unmold the soufflés into the gratin dish. Put in a medium oven until they double in size.

Serve with a boiling sauce of mushrooms, shellfish, *Sauce Nantua* (page 259)—or simply hot melted butter and parsley.

♈ Dry light white, Mâcon, white Hermitage

QUENELLES DE BROCHET

PIKE QUENELLES

A proper mix for a quenelle is almost impossible to achieve in a kitchen that does not have the right equipment. This recipe is from memory, but it is easier to buy quenelles—truffled or not—from a specialist. Choose quenelles of around three ounces per person.

This dish must not wait for the guests to finish their preceding course. La Mère would go into a terrible temper on the subject, and very often she would start this dish all over again, because the guests were not ready to be served.

FOR 10 LARGE
  QUENELLES:
1 ¼ CUPS MILK
2 CUPS FLOUR
1 ¼ CUPS BUTTER
9 OZ PIKE
8 EGGS
SALT
PEPPER
NUTMEG

Make a good paste, moistened well, with the milk, the flour, and ¼ cup of the butter . . . leave to cool. Put through a meat grinder with a very fine mesh.

Incorporate into the mix 1 cup butter, the flesh of the pike, the whole eggs, salt, pepper, and nutmeg to your taste. Work for 30 minutes.

Make small quenelles with a tablespoon and simmer in salted water for a good quarter of an hour.

Place each quenelle in a gratin dish with the sauce—see below. The sauce must be boiling. Leave to cook for 30 minutes in a hot oven.

SAUCE POUR LES QUENELLES

SAUCE FOR QUENELLES

FOR 10 QUENELLES:
2 PINTS WHOLE MILK
BEURRE MANIÉ
  (PAGE 254)
1 CUP HEAVY CREAM
SALT
PEPPER
1 LB MUSHROOMS
BUTTER
1 SPOON FLOUR OR
  CORNSTARCH

Bring the milk to a boil. Bind with the *beurre manié*. Don't let it get too thick. Add the cream and the seasoning. Add in sliced mushrooms and bring back to a boil . . . taste! Pour into a gratin dish big enough that the quenelles can double in volume.

Optional: Leftover *sauce américaine* (a *velouté* flavored with lobster shells) and a few pieces of lobster can replace the mushrooms.

♀ Young white Mâcon, Pouilly-Fuissé, Pouilly-Fumé

FILETS DE SOLE EN COCONS

SOLE IN BLANKETS

This recipe is previously unpublished. It comes from the imagination of a great, little-known chef, M. Menweg, owner of The Fillet of Sole restaurant in Lyon, long since lost. We give the recipe here as a reminder of how his fish used to be done.

1 (1-LB) SOLE
1 PIECE MONKFISH
3.5 OZ MUSHROOMS
SHALLOTS
SALT
PEPPER
FLOUR
9 OZ QUENELLES DE
   BROCHET (PAGE 51)
BUTTER

Take off the 4 fillets from the sole and flatten on a board. For the hash, chop together the monkfish, the mushrooms, and the shallots. Cook together for a few minutes; salt and pepper. Spread this mix over the fillets of sole and fold them over on themselves.

Roll out the *quenelles de brochet* on a floured surface, until big enough to enclose the fillets. Wrap each fillet in the mix so it is tucked up in a blanket. Put the parcels on to poach by dropping them carefully into a casserole of boiling salted water. Leave to simmer for 20 minutes.

Lift out the sole parcels using a skimmer, and put on a napkin. This first part of the preparation can all be done the night before.

To cook your parcels, put them in a well-buttered gratin dish with a big piece of butter. Add a glass of salted water. Bake in a hot oven for 15 to 20 minutes. They should be well colored.

They can be served as they are with their cooking liquid or, for a more refined dish, with a lobster sauce, or *Sauce Nantua* (page 259).

♆ Pouilly-Fuissé, Pouilly-Fumé

LA MÈRE'S
CLASSIC MENU NO. 1

Fonds d'Artichauts au Foie Gras

Artichokes with Foie Gras

(page 56)

◆

Langouste Belle Aurore

Lobster with Brandy and Cream

(page 98)

◆

Volaille Demi-Deuil

Chicken in Half-mourning (page 142)

◆

Fromages Assortis

Assorted Cheeses

◆

Tous les Desserts

Dessert of Your Choice

HORS-D'OEUVRES ET ENTRÉES
STARTERS AND
FIRST COURSES

FONDS D'ARTICHAUTS PÉRIGOURDINE

ARTICHOKES WITH TRUFFLES

Artichokes should be served with hot toast, either as an hors d'oeuvre or after a roast, if it is a light meal. The only difficult part is twisting off the chokes of the artichokes. To do this, you need a knife that is as sharp as a razor, short, and pointed.

Tear open the main leaves of the artichoke, don't cut them. Cut off the bottom leaves, removing all the green parts. Trim the side leaves to the desired height. Remove the choke with a knife, leaving just the flesh. Place this immediately into cold water with lemon.

1 ARTICHOKE
  PER PERSON
LEMON
SAUCE VINAIGRETTE
  (PAGE 264)
SEASONAL SALAD
SALT
PEPPER
TRUFFLES
WALNUTS
PARSLEY
BAYONNE HAM
  (OPTIONAL)

Put the artichokes in a large pan of water and bring to a boil—the water should be cold to start, and without any lemon. (Contrary to what people often think, lemon has an unpleasant taste when cooked.) The artichokes are cooked when you can pierce them easily with a fork.

Leave them in water until they are to be used.

Remove the artichokes 15 minutes before service, dry them with a tea towel, and leave them to marinate in the vinaigrette.

Remove them after 15 minutes and place them on an earthenware or porcelain plate on top of a bed of seasonal salad, already seasoned. Top with julienne of truffles, walnuts, and a sprinkle of chopped parsley. You can also add a small amount of Bayonne ham.

FONDS D'ARTICHAUTS AU FOIE GRAS: Follow the above recipe, garnishing the artichokes with a slice of cold foie gras.

Serve with very hot toast.

STOFINADO

SALT COD PUREE

Etymologically, stofinado *(stockfish) is a fish dried on poles (the stocks).*

SALT COD
NUT OIL
4 OR 5 EGGS
1 CUP HEAVY CREAM
SALT
PEPPER
PARSLEY
GARLIC

Soak the salt cod for 24 hours in clean water, changing the water frequently.

Drain, wipe dry, and cut the fish into thin slices as for smoked salmon. Warm some nut oil in a pan and put the fish on to cook, stirring with a wooden spoon all the time to get a white puree.

Beat the eggs with the heavy cream; salt and pepper. Add to the fish and leave for a few minutes.

At the moment of service (when it is very hot) sprinkle over a large spoon of chopped parsley and 2 crushed cloves of garlic.

♀ White Mâcon

PÂTE FEUILLETÉE

PUFF PASTRY

This pastry can be kept in the refrigerator once it has been turned four times. To use, leave to warm up and give it two more turns. Traditionally, the pastry is rolled into a flat rectangle, then turned four times counterclockwise, and folded back over itself into neat threes. Premade puff pastry is readily available in most supermarkets these days.

5 CUPS FLOUR
2 TEASPOONS SALT
2 ½ CUPS BUTTER

Sift the flour onto marble or a table. Make a well. Add the salt, and 1 ¼ cups water, and start to knead so the flour absorbs all the liquid. The pâte should be firm and elastic. Some flours absorb more liquid than others.

Roll out the pâte into a rectangle with a thickness of ¾ inch. Cream the butter with your fingers so that it has the same consistency as the pâte, and spread it across the pâte. Fold in the 4 edges to enclose the butter inside. Roll out on the marble and repeat the action 3 times.

Turn a quarter turn and start again. Leave to stand for an hour.

Roll out and turn twice more, and leave to stand for another hour. Roll out again, twice, before it is ready, repeating the same actions.

Carefully dust off any surplus flour and fold the pâte over on itself again.

LES BOUCHÉES

CANAPÉS

Bouchées *(meaning "mouthfuls"—sometimes called* barquettes *or small tarts depending on the shape) are small croutons made with* pâte feuilletée *(puff pastry). You can buy them in the shops and put them straight into the oven with their garnish. However, they are always better made at home. You can also put the fillings into ovenproof porcelain molds, which is quicker and avoids making the* pâte feuilletée.

PÂTE FEUILLETÉE
(OPPOSITE)
EGG

Roll out the *pâte feuilletée* to ⅔ inch thick, and cut out round pouches about 3 ¼ inches in diameter. Wash with beaten egg. Mark the top with the point of a knife. Cook in a hot oven for about 15 minutes.

They can be filled in an infinite number of ways with vegetables, meat, fish, shellfish, and so on. Let your imagination run riot!

RICE: Cooked rice with crushed tomatoes and chopped bell peppers.

CHICKEN: Cut into small dice, bound with a thick chicken *velouté* with cream.

FISH: A *salpicon* of diced fish mixed with chopped mushrooms and *Sauce Normande* (page 260), warmed in the oven.

OYSTERS: Poached, strained, and trimmed oysters sauced with Mornay, sprinkled with butter, and warmed under the broiler.

CHAUSSONS AUX TRUFFES

TRUFFLE TURNOVERS

TRUFFLES
SALT
PEPPER
SPICES (PEPPER,
  CLOVES, NUTMEG,
  CINNAMON)
LARD FAT OR BACON
PÂTE FEUILLETÉE
  (PAGE 58)
EGG YOLK

Peel some medium (nut-sized) truffles. Salt lightly, add a touch of pepper and spices. Wrap each one around with a fine slice of lard fat or bacon, unsalted.

Cut from a sheet of *pâte feuilletée* of ¹⁄₁₆ inch thickness, some rounds 2 ¾ to 3 inches in diameter. Seal the truffles in their shirts of lard inside the sheets of pâte, having made sure to moisten the edges so they seal well.

Lay in a dish and wash with egg yolk. Bake for 20 to 30 minutes in a hot oven and serve immediately.

♆ Pouilly-Fuissé, Pouilly-Fumé, Alsace

PÂTE À BRIOCHE

BRIOCHE DOUGH

For the yeast we recommend one and a half to two teaspoons in summer and 1 tablespoon in winter. Add a quarter of a cup sugar for a sweet dough.

5 CUPS FLOUR
1 TABLESPOON SALT
6 EGGS
½ GLASS MILK
1 ½ TO 2 CUPS FINE
  BUTTER
YEAST

Make the pâte the night before, around 4 p.m.

Sift the flour into a big enough bowl. Add the salt, sugar, eggs, and yeast dissolved in warm milk. Work in the mixer.

After a few minutes, add the creamed butter. Keep working for another 15 minutes to give the pâte maximum body. Leave to rise in a warm atmosphere, uncovered and open to currents of air, for 2 hours.

Work again for 2 to 3 minutes. Cover the mix and leave out in the open air, or in the refrigerator in summer.

The next day, work the pâte again a little. Season if you wish (depending on the occasion) and leave to rise again in the warm atmosphere.

Bake in a hot oven for 25 minutes.

SAUCISSON EN FEUILLETAGE OU EN BRIOCHE

SAUSAGE IN PASTRY

Pâte feuilletée is more delicate and less filling than pâte à brioche. This dish is well known around Lyon—the problem is finding sausage of the best quality. Do not prick the sausage (as is often done).

SAUSAGE
SALT
PÂTE FEUILLETÉE
  (PAGE 58)
OR PÂTE À BRIOCHE
  (OPPOSITE)
EGG YOLK

Simmer the sausage in salted water, just enough to cover. Simmer gently for about 15 minutes without letting it boil. Lift the sausage out before it is quite cooked and take off the skin.

Wrap the sausage meat in a sheet of *pâte feuilletée* about ⅛ inch thick. Paint with egg yolk and bake in a medium oven for about 30 minutes.

If using *pâte à brioche*, wrap the sausage meat in a brioche mix about a ½ inch thick. Place in a warm area away from any drafts. Leave to rise for 1 hour. Paint with egg yolk and bake in a medium oven for about 30 minutes.

♀ Pouilly-Fumé, white Mâcon, Alsace

FOIE GRAS EN BRIOCHE

FOIE GRAS IN BRIOCHE

FOIE GRAS AU
  NATUREL (PAGE 62)
PÂTE À BRIOCHE
  (OPPOSITE)
SALT
PEPPER

Prepare the *Foie Gras au Naturel*—but do not cook it quite so long. Leave to cool and take off carefully all traces of fat.

Line an oval mold or one just longer than the foie gras with *pâte à brioche*, unsweetened. Make sure the sides are high enough that pâte does not overlap them. Lay the foie gras on the pâte, fold over the rest of the pâte and leave to rise in the open air until the pâte has doubled in volume. Bake in a medium oven for 40 to 45 minutes.

Serve hot or cold, as you prefer.

♀ Alsace, Champagne

FOIE GRAS AU NATUREL

GOOSE OR DUCK LIVER

Goose liver is more delicate, more elegant than duck liver, which you might call more rustic.

1 (1.75-LB) FRESH
  GOOSE OR DUCK
  LIVER
SPICES (PEPPER,
  CLOVES, NUTMEG,
  CINNAMON)
SALT
PEPPER
1 GLASS COGNAC
1 GLASS PORT
GOOSE FAT
  (OPTIONAL)
LARD
TRUFFLE

Choose a firm liver, lightly pink. Take off all traces of sinew and veins. Put it in a terrine with spices, salt, pepper, Cognac, and port. Leave to macerate for a few hours, turning the liver.

Wipe dry and put in a casserole with a thick bottom, with or without the goose fat, but cook very gently. Allow about 40 minutes. A knitting needle inserted into the liver should come out without any traces of blood.

Leave to cool and, when the fat has taken well, place the liver on a layer of lard in a terrine. Hermetically seal and keep in the cold.

To serve, trim off all the fat, cut into slices, and decorate with slices of truffle.

℞ Chablis, Meursault, Alsace

ESCALOPES DE FOIE GRAS FRAIS BRILLAT-SAVARIN

FOIE GRAS BRILLAT-SAVARIN

Can also be served with Les Bouchées *filled with creamed mushrooms (page 59).*

1 FRESH GOOSE
  OR DUCK LIVER
TRUFFLES
BUTTER
BREAD
1 EGG
OIL
SALT
PEPPER

Cut the liver into slightly thick scallops. Make a lengthways cut into the scallops. Fry some slices of fresh truffle in butter and then place them inside the cuts in the liver.

Close up the scallops like sandwiches and dip in *à l'anglaise*—a beaten egg, a spoon of water, a spoon of oil, a pinch of salt, and a little pepper. Cook in butter over a gentle flame.

Arrange on thin croutons of bread fried in butter.

℞ Alsace, Chablis, Meursault, Champagne

PÂTÉ DE FOIE GRAS FAÇON STRASBOURG

STRASBOURG PÂTÉ OF FOIE GRAS

14 OZ FILLET
   OF PORK
2¼ CUPS FRESH
   GOOSE FAT
5 OZ FRESH GOOSE
   OR DUCK LIVER
   TRIMMINGS
SALT
PEPPER
SPICES (PEPPER,
   CLOVES, NUTMEG,
   CINNAMON)
1 GLASS PORT
1 GLASS MADEIRA
1 GLASS COGNAC
1 (1.75-LB) GOOSE
   OR DUCK LIVER
TRUFFLES
PÂTE À BRIOCHE
   (PAGE 60)
EGG YOLK
ASPIC JELLY
   (PAGE 267)

In a blender, grind the pork, fat, and liver trimmings to get a very smooth paste. Add salt, pepper, spices, port, Madeira, Cognac. Mix everything well together.

Trim the whole liver and adorn with fresh truffles.

Line a tall, oval pâté mold with a layer of *pâte à brioche*, rolled out to ⅛ inch thick. Fill with half the ground meats. Lay the whole liver in the middle and cover with the rest of the meat. Cram it in tight. Cover over with the brioche dough and seal the edges with water, turning them over to create a small border. Make a small chimney in the middle with parchment paper. Wash with the yolk of an egg. Bake in a medium oven. Allow 30 minutes for each 2.2 pounds of meat.

When the pâté has cooled, pour into the pâté—down its chimney—a good-quality aspic jelly enriched with Madeira and port.

♈ Riesling

POMPONNETTES DE FOIE GRAS

FOIE GRAS POMPOMS

2 ½ CUPS FLOUR
PINCH OF SALT
¼ CUP ALMONDS
¾ CUPS BUTTER,
  MELTED
4 EGGS
7 OZ FRESH GOOSE
  OR DUCK LIVER
2 SPOONS CHOPPED
  TRUFFLE
PISTACHIO NUTS
OIL FOR FRYING

Make a pastry with the flour, salt, roasted and chopped almonds, melted butter, eggs, and ½ cup water. Knead everything together with your fingertips and punch it down twice as for making *Pâte Brisée* (page 82). Leave to rest 2 hours.

Force the liver through a sieve. Take one-third of this puree and add the chopped truffle. Make 20 little balls from this mix and insert into each one a shelled pistachio.

Wrap these truffled nuts of liver inside an envelope of the remaining liver puree.

Roll out the pastry to ⅛ inch thick and cut into rounds of about 3 ¼ inches. Moisten the edges and seal up the liver nuts inside. Fry for a few minutes in boiling oil.

Serve very hot on a napkin.

♀ Port, Alsace

CAILLETTES DE L'ARDÈCHE

LITTLE BIRDS OF ARDÈCHE

1 LB SWISS CHARD
3.5 OZ SPINACH
1 STALK CELERY
5 OZ PORK LIVER
5 OZ SAUSAGE MEAT
SALT
PEPPER
ALLSPICE
DRIED BASIL AND
  THYME
SAUSAGE SKINS
BUTTER OR LARD

Swiss chard is related to beet, but we only eat the stalks and leaves.

Blanch the Swiss chard, spinach, and celery. Chop the vegetables with the pork liver and mix up well with the sausage meat. Season with salt, pepper, allspice, dried basil, and thyme. Knead it all together well.

Make little balls and enclose in sausage skins. Cook in a well-buttered dish in a gentle oven for about 20 minutes.

These are eaten very hot with a good puree of potato, or cold.

♀ A light Côtes-du-Rhône

LA MÈRE'S
CLASSIC MENU No.2

Huîtres de Belon
Belon Oysters

◆

Saumon Fumé
Smoked Salmon

◆

Poularde de Bresse "Mère Brazier"
Bresse Hen "Mère Brazier"

◆

Pâté Foie Gras façon Strasbourg
Strasbourg Pâté of Foie Gras (page 63)

◆

Salade de Scarole
Chicory Salad

◆

Bombe Glacée aux Ananas Frais
Bombe Ice Cream with Fresh Pineapple

GRATINÉE LYONNAISE

ONION SOUP

7 OZ ONION
BUTTER
2 QUARTS CHICKEN
  STOCK
BAGUETTE
GRUYÈRE CHEESE
3 OR 4 EGG YOLKS
  (OPTIONAL)
1 GLASS PORT
  (OPTIONAL)

Warm through in butter finely chopped onions. Leave to color and then cover with stock or the juices from a *pot au feu* (you can top up with some water). Leave to cook for 10 minutes.

While it is cooking, cut some rounds from a baguette and allow to dry in the oven until they are lightly colored.

Put the rounds of bread in an ovenproof soup tureen. Alternate a layer of sliced bread and a layer of grated Gruyère . . . and then another. Pour over the stock, strained or not, as you prefer. Put in a hot oven for 30 minutes to brown.

You can serve the soup as it is, or to improve it, mix in, as it comes out of the oven, 3 or 4 egg yolks whisked together with a glass of port. Slip this mix into the soup—under the croutons—and mix into the stock.

Serve in hot tureens with grated Gruyère on the table.

♉ White Mâcon, Beaujolais nouveau, port

PRUNEAUX FARCIS

STUFFED PRUNES

Agen prunes come from the southwest of France. They are the most famous variety of prunes and are available worldwide.

AGEN PRUNES
RICE
BEER
CHICKEN STOCK
ALMONDS

Soak some Agen prunes in warm water. Drain and wipe dry. Simmer them in chicken stock—10 minutes should be enough. Drain them and take out the stones. Reduce the cooking liquid until you have a syrup.

Make a risotto using half beer and half chicken stock.

Stuff the prunes with the risotto. Arrange them in a gratin dish and pour over the syrup. Put them in a hot oven for a few minutes, then serve them garnished with chopped roasted almonds.

♉ Beer

CHAMPIGNONS FARCIS

STUFFED MUSHROOMS

La Mère specifies godiveau forcemeat, a traditional pâté or fresh sausage that is served hot and made with beef and andouillette or belly fat. She would always serve these as starters for the annual November 11 celebrations.

12 LARGE
 MUSHROOMS
GODIVEAU
 FORCEMEAT
BUTTER
2 SHALLOTS
FLOUR
1 GLASS DRY
 WHITE WINE
SALT
PEPPER

Clean the mushrooms carefully. Take out the stalks and fill with the forcemeat.

Finely chop the mushroom stalks and warm through in butter with 2 chopped shallots. As it starts to color, sprinkle with a spoon of flour. Moisten with white wine. Salt and pepper, and let it reduce for a few minutes.

Dip the mushrooms in flour and color in some butter in a pan, stuffed side up. Arrange in a buttered dish, stuffed side up, cover with the shallot mix, and put in a hot oven for a few minutes. Serve very hot, on hot plates.

♀ Muscadet, rosé

CHESTER CAKE

LANCASHIRE CHEESE CAKE

Lancashire is an English cheese made from cow's milk.

1½ CUPS FLOUR
⅓ CUP BUTTER
1¼ CUPS GRATED
 LANCASHIRE
 CHEESE
3 EGG YOLKS
SAUCE BÉCHAMEL
 (PAGE 255)
SALT
CAYENNE PEPPER

Make a good, well-mixed, quite-thick dough with the flour, butter, ⅔ cup of grated Lancashire cheese, and 2 egg yolks.

Roll out the pâte to about ⅕ inch thick. Cut out small circular galette shapes. Wash with egg yolk. Bake in a hot oven for about 15 minutes.

You can serve these galettes as sandwiches with a puree in the middle, made of a cup of thick béchamel, an egg yolk, the remaining cheese, a nut of butter, salt, and cayenne pepper.

♀ Beer, white wine

CRÊPES FARCIES GRATINÉES

STUFFED CRÊPES

Children usually enjoy this kind of dish. The stuffings can vary according to what you have as leftovers. As with all these kinds of starters, you can give free rein to your imagination, which often produces excellent results . . . Or try the following: Antiboise are dice of fresh tuna with chopped hard-boiled egg, bound with Sauce Béchamel and a Beurre d'Anchois (Anchovy Butter, page 252); Indienne are chopped onions cooked in butter, plus chopped sautéed mushrooms; bind with a béchamel seasoned with curry powder. For Périgourdine, make a puree of goose or duck liver, mixed with chopped truffles.

PÂTE A CRÊPES
(PAGE 234)
CHOPPED CHICKEN,
MEAT, OR FISH
MUSHROOMS
SAUCE BÉCHAMEL
(PAGE 255)
BUTTER
GRUYÈRE CHEESE

Make some little crêpes with an unsweetened batter.

Fill them with chopped leftover chicken, white meat, or fish. Add in some chopped mushrooms and bind with the béchamel.

Place the crêpes in a gratin dish, pour over some *sauce béchamel* well thickened with cream, and sprinkle over some grated Gruyère. Gratinate in a hot oven and serve very hot.

♀ White, rosé

CRÊPES AUX TRUFFES

TRUFFLE CRÊPES

FOR 15 CRÊPES:
1½ CUPS FLOUR
3 PINCHES OF SALT
2 EGGS
2 CUPS MILK
1 FRESH TRUFFLE
4 SOUPSPOONS OF
TRUFFLE JUS
BUTTER

Make a well in the flour in a bowl, add the salt and eggs. Mix everything together to get a smooth batter. Pour in the milk and mix. Pass through a sieve to be sure to have a pâte without lumps. Leave to stand for an hour.

Cut the truffle into julienne—thin matchsticks—and incorporate with its juice into the batter.

Butter a frying pan and pour in enough batter to cover. Cook until set.

POUNTARI AUVERGNAT

AUVERGNE POUNTARI

10 OZ PORK BELLY
1 ONION
PARSLEY
7 OZ BLANCHED
   SWISS CHARD
MILK
FLOUR
2 EGGS
SALT
PEPPER
BUTTER

In a grinder, make a good compact mixture of the pork belly, onion, parsley, and Swiss chard.

Make a batter with milk, flour, and eggs—as if making crêpe batter, but thicker. Salt, pepper, and add in the meat and chard mixture. Pour this mix into a lightly buttered cocotte and cook in the oven for about 1 hour.

The *pountari* is cooked when a golden crust forms around the edges of the cocotte. Eat hot.

♟ White, red

BLINIS

BLINIS

Blinis are cooked like crêpes—in a small pan—but made a little thicker than a pancake and cooked a little longer, so they have a light crust. They can be served with caviar, smoked salmon, fresh butter, or thick cream.

1 SPOON BEER YEAST
2 CUPS MILK
5 CUPS FLOUR
1½ CUPS BUCKWHEAT
   FLOUR
3 EGGS, SEPARATED
SALT
SUGAR
¾ CUP BUTTER

Dissolve the yeast in the milk. Add a mix of both flours. Knead with 3 egg yolks. Salt a little, sugar, and mix in the melted butter.

Whisk the egg whites into snow and fold into the mix. Leave to rest overnight.

♟ Vodka, Champagne, light Alsace, light beer

CRAPIAUX MORVANDIAUX

POTATO PANCAKES

These pancakes can be eaten hot or cold. They are recommended as starters if the menu is a little light.

3 POTATOES
3 TABLESPOONS
  FLOUR
3 EGGS
MILK
SALT
OIL

Grate the potatoes. Add the flour, eggs, and a little milk, and salt lightly. Work carefully so you have a batter slightly thicker than for making pancakes.

Warm the oil in a big enough pan to get a pancake ⅕ inch thick. Leave to cook well before turning over and cooking on.

Ⴤ Dry white, rosé

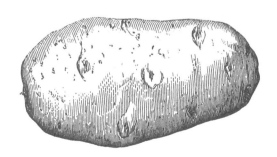

ESCARGOTS DE BOURGOGNE

BURGUNDY SNAILS

When the snails are very hot, before serving, you can pour on a little dry white wine . . .

100 SNAILS
SEA SALT
1 BOTTLE DRY WHITE
   WINE
CARROTS
ONIONS
PARSLEY STALKS
CHERVIL
BOUQUET GARNI
2 CLOVES GARLIC
PEPPERCORNS
BEURRE D'ESCARGOTS
   (PAGE 253)

The night before, carefully wash the snails, salt well with sea salt. Cover and leave overnight. Make the *beurre d'escargots*.

The next day wash the snails in enough changes of clean water until there is no salt or scum left. Plunge them into a large marmite of boiling water. Cook for 5 minutes.

Leave to cool until they can be handled one by one. Take them out of their shells with a snail fork. Lift off the black vein. Wash again in clean water and leave to drain in a sieve.

Make a court bouillon with the white wine, chopped carrots, onions, parsley stalks, chervil, bouquet garni, garlic, and peppercorns. Add in the snails. Cook for at least 2 hours.

Strain and drain the snails and dry in a cloth. Put a nut of snail butter back in each shell, then a snail, and then plug with more butter.

To serve, put in a hot oven for a few minutes, until the butter melts.

(Over) La Mère joints a chicken   71

PÂTE À NOUILLES

FRESH PASTA

FLOUR
EGGS
BUTTER
SALT
PEPPER

Pour the flour into a mountain on the table. Put in the middle a pinch of salt, 2 whole eggs, 2 egg yolks, and the butter, and knead everything together. Keep in the open air, wrapped in a linen cloth, for at least 2 hours.

Roll out as thin as a piece of paper, fold over, and cut into thin slices, flouring as you go.

Shake off the excess flour and put into boiling water—about 10 minutes.

BEURRECKS À LA TURQUE

TURKISH CIGARS

The "Turks"—the edges are turned up like a sultan's shoes—are mentioned also by Escoffier.

GRUYÈRE CHEESE
SAUCE BÉCHAMEL
 (PAGE 255)
PÂTE À NOUILLES
 (ABOVE)
EGGS
BREAD CRUMBS

Put the Gruyère in a thick béchamel sauce. Mix well and allow to cool until it is cold. Roll it out and cut into small cylinders 6 inches long. Wrap each piece in a thin layer of pasta dough. Seal with egg and roll in fresh bread crumbs.

Deep-fry and turn out on absorbent paper, and serve very hot.

♀ Alsace, white Mâcon

PÂTE À CHOUX

CHOUX PASTRY DOUGH

1 TABLESPOON SALT
2 TABLESPOONS
     SUGAR (OPTIONAL)
1 CUP BUTTER
3 CUPS FLOUR
12 EGGS

In a thick-bottomed casserole, warm 2 cups of water with the salt. Add the butter, and then, as it comes to a boil, add the sifted flour in one go. Stir hard with a wooden spoon until the dough is well homogenized and leaves the sides of the pan.

Leave it to cool a little and incorporate, one at a time, the whole eggs, stirring all the time. Leave the dough for an hour to rest.

GNOCCHIS À LA PARISIENNE

PARISIAN GNOCCHI

In Italian, gnocco, *the singular of* gnocchi, *means "little bread."*

PÂTE À CHOUX
MASHED POTATO
PARMESAN CHEESE
SAUCE BÉCHAMEL
     (PAGE 255)
BUTTER

Add to the choux pastry batter one-fifth its own weight of both mashed potatoes and Parmesan. Knead well.

Using a piping tip ¾ inch in diameter, squeeze out little sausages 1 ¼ inches long, and drop them into a casserole of boiling salted water. Leave to poach for a few minutes. Lift out and drain on a towel. Put them in a gratin dish and sauce with béchamel.

Sprinkle with grated Parmesan and put in a warm oven. You can top the Parmesan with a few nuts of butter.

♉ White, rosé

GNOCCHIS À LA ROMAINE

ROMAN GNOCCHI

1 QUART MILK
SALT
NUTMEG
⅓ CUP BUTTER
1⅛ CUPS DURUM
    WHEAT FLOUR
1 EGG
PARMESAN OR
    GRUYÈRE CHEESE

Bring the milk to a boil with salt and a grating of nutmeg. Add the butter, sprinkle the flour like rain into the boiling milk. Whisk energetically and finish with a wooden spoon, because the mixture has a tendency to stick to the bottom of the casserole. Away from the heat, add the egg and a spoon of grated Parmesan. The mix should be even and smooth.

Pour out onto a flat surface, or—better—a buttered marble work board. Roll out to a thickness of about ¾ inch. Leave to cool. Cut up into rectangles or circles.

Arrange in a buttered gratin dish, generously garnished with grated Parmesan (or Gruyère). Add a nut of butter and gratinate in a hot oven.

♇ Côtes-du-Rhône rosé

MIGNONNES BRIOCHES FARCIES

CHEESE BRIOCHES

These brioches are usually served covered with a napkin to keep them warm.

PÂTE À BRIOCHE
    (PAGE 60) OR
    PÂTE À CHOUX
    (PAGE 75)
GRUYÈRE, COMTÉ,
    PARMESAN, OR
    ROQUEFORT
SAUCE SUPRÊME
    (PAGE 263)

Make little brioche cakes similar in size and shape to that of a profiterole. You could use other forms of batter, unsweetened.

When the brioches are baked, take off the hats and scoop out some space in each cake. Let them dry out a little in the oven and then garnish with a very thick *sauce suprême* and fill with Gruyère, Parmesan, Comté, or Roquefort. Put their hats back on and warm in a gentle oven.

♇ Any white wine, Champagne

GRATIN DE MACARONIS FAÇON MÈRE BRAZIER

MÈRE BRAZIER'S MACARONI AND CHEESE

This simple dish was often ordered at the restaurant by regulars, even when they were entertaining important clients. You must have excellent-quality fat macaroni, which is not always easy to find in France.

MACARONI
BUTTER
MILK
SAUCE BÉCHAMEL
   (PAGE 255)
SALT
PEPPER
HEAVY CREAM
GRUYÈRE CHEESE

Break the macaroni into pieces 2 to 3 inches long. Put them on to cook in salted water until still quite firm. Drain and keep warm in some hot milk.

Make a little béchamel sauce, not too thick. Salt, pepper, and add the same volume of cream.

Put this sauce in a porcelain gratin dish on the fire. Drain the macaroni pieces and add them. Spread over generously some freshly grated Gruyère and add a nut of butter. Move to a medium oven to color slowly and serve when it starts to bubble.

GRATIN DAUPHINOIS FAÇON MÈRE BRAZIER

MÈRE BRAZIER'S DAUPHINOIS POTATOES

We don't subscribe to using egg, which would give the gratin the style of a flan. Many chefs do, however—it is a question of taste. Use enough potatoes to fill an ovenproof dish. Cooking time depends on the thickness of the potato slices.

POTATOES
2 CUPS MILK
GARLIC
SALT
PEPPER
HEAVY CREAM
BUTTER

Carefully peel some good, yellow-fleshed potatoes of medium size. Bring the milk to a boil.

Slice the potatoes into thin rounds, add to the milk, and pour everything into a stone, earthenware, or porcelain dish that you have already rubbed with garlic.

Salt, pepper, and add a few tablespoons of heavy cream and a few nuts of butter. Put in the oven until cooked, which you can check by pushing in the blade of a knife.

FONDUE SAVOYARDE

SAVOY FONDUE

Well known and fashionable in the Rhônes-Alpes, you need the famous earthenware caquelon *dish (with a thick bottom so it does not burn over an open-spirit flame). Everyone helps themselves with a cube of bread on the end of a fork with a long handle. Don't forget the drinks, or the guests will die of thirst!*

DRY WHITE WINE
  FROM SAVOY
COMTÉ CHEESE
BEAUFORT CHEESE
EMMENTAL CHEESE
TRUFFLES (OPTIONAL)
KIRSCH (OPTIONAL)
BREAD

Warm some dry white Savoy wine—enough for the number of guests.

Cut slices, in equal parts, of cheese—Comté, Beaufort, and Emmental. Lay into the wine and mix slowly over a low heat to get a smooth and loose paste. You can add in truffles and kirsch.

To serve, place the *caquelon* on a warming plate with an open flame.

♇ Crépy

FONDUE À L'ANCIENNE

TRADITIONAL FONDUE

Serve like a Fondue Savoyarde *(above) or eat from the hot pan.*

EGGS
GRUYÈRE CHEESE
BUTTER
SALT
PEPPER

Allow 2 eggs per person and some very good grated Gruyère (one-third the weight of the eggs). Beat the eggs in an earthenware casserole and add in the Gruyère and a piece of butter of about one-sixth the weight of the eggs.

Put the casserole on a very low heat and mix with a wooden spoon to get a creamy, thin liquid. Check the seasoning with salt and a grind of pepper.

♇ Pouilly, Crépy

JAMBON AU CINZANO DRY

HAM IN CINZANO

HAM ON THE BONE
CINZANO DRY
MADEIRA
MUSHROOMS
SAUCE BÉCHAMEL
  (PAGE 255)
SALT
PEPPER
BUTTER

On a buttered plate, lay out a good slice of ham (1 per person). Moisten with a mix of 2 parts of Cinzano dry and 1 of Madeira—just enough to cover. Leave to marinate for 1 hour.

Slice the mushrooms and sweat through in butter. Prepare a well-colored béchamel. Season with salt and pepper.

Cover the ham with buttered, ovenproof paper and put in the oven for a few minutes to start to reduce.

Lift off the paper, cover with the mushrooms and a layer of béchamel. Raise to the top of a red-hot oven to color.

Serve with leaf spinach, sweated in butter.

♀ Light white, Côtes-du-Rhône rosé

TANCHE OU CARPE FARCIE À LA MORVANDELLE

TENCH OR CARP MORVANDE

6.5 LB TENCH OR
  CARP
PÂTE À CHOUX (PAGE
  75)
GRUYÈRE CHEESE
DRY WHITE WINE
SALT
PEPPER
BUTTER
BREAD CRUMBS

Let the fish rest in fresh water to cleanse for a good time, then take off the larger scales. Split open down the whole length of the back and lift out the main bone and any others you can. Gut.

Stuff with an unsweetened *pâte à choux* mixed with the Gruyère, cut up into big dice. Sew up the fish with strong cotton. Place in a well-buttered gratin dish. Scatter the bread crumbs over. Cover with dry white wine. Salt and pepper. Cook in a gentle oven for about 2 hours.

You can hold back some of the *pâte à choux* to make some small gnocchi to go round the fish 10 minutes before the end of the cooking. Serve at the last minute, very hot.

♀ Pouilly-Fuissé, Sancerre

MARENNES GRATINÉES À LA FAVORITE

GRATIN OF OYSTERS

When opening the oysters, be careful to keep all the juices. Oysters from the Marennes-Oléron, raised under very strict controls, are always of a very high quality, but any variety of oyster will be okay for this recipe.

BUTTER
1 SHALLOT
1 GLASS MUSCADET
    OR OTHER DRY
    WHITE WINE
1 LEMON
12 MARENNES-
    OLÉRON OYSTERS
BEURRE MANIÉ
    (PAGE 254)
2 EGG YOLKS
2 SPOONS HEAVY
    CREAM
12 MUSHROOMS
BREAD CRUMBS
GRUYÈRE CHEESE

In a small pan, warm in butter 1 finely chopped shallot. Add the dry white wine, a little butter, the juice of the lemon, and the liquor from the oysters. Poach the oysters in this liquid for 7 or 8 minutes.

Take out the oysters. Bind the cooking liquid with the *beurre manié*. Add the egg yolks and heavy cream.

Separately, finely chop the mushrooms and sweat in butter. Fill the oyster shells. Top with an oyster for each shell. Pour the sauce over. Sprinkle over some bread crumbs and grated Gruyère. Put in the top of a very hot oven for a few minutes.

♀ Muscadet, Sancerre

PÂTE POUR PÂTÉ EN CROÛTE

PASTRY FOR ENCASING

5 CUPS FLOUR
4 EGG YOLKS
6½ CUPS BUTTER
4 TEASPOONS SALT

Sift the flour. Make a well in the middle and break in the egg yolks, melted butter, salt, and 1 ¾ cups of water. Knead well and work a few minutes.

Punch it—which is to say, punch it with the heel of your hand—3 or 4 times to give it plenty of body. In practice, it will have to be strong enough to support the meat, to resist the heat of cooking and the introduction of a hot gelatin.

PÂTE BRISÉE

SHORT PASTRY

This recipe serves as a base for flans, quiches . . .

FOR ONE TART OF
  EIGHT PORTIONS:
5 CUPS FLOUR
2 TEASPOONS SALT
3 EGGS
1 CUP BUTTER

Sift the flour onto a marble surface or a table. Make a well in the middle. Add salt, eggs, and melted butter.

Work with your fingertips to ensure a homogenous mix. Bash it 3 times, which is to say smash the dough under the palm of your hand. Gather it up into a ball, wrap in linen, and leave out until the next day.

PÂTÉ CHAUD DE GIBIER, BÉCASSE, FAISAN, GRIVE

HOT GAME PÂTÉ

We prefer Pâte pour Pâté en Croûte *(opposite) to* Pâte Feuilletée *(page 58) for terrines en croute made in molds. Even so, you can use* pâte pour pâté en croûte *to line the mold and make a covering with* pâte feuilletée. *The pastry is best made the night before and left out, covered with clean linen.*

GAME (WOODCOCK,
    PHEASANT,
    LARK, ETC.)
CARROTS
ONION
PORK
1 OR 2 EGG YOLKS
1 SPOON FLOUR
SALT
PEPPER
1 GLASS COGNAC
1 GLASS MADEIRA
PÂTE POUR PÂTÉ EN
    CROÛTE (OPPOSITE)
FRESH GOOSE OR
    DUCK LIVER
TRUFFLE

Debone the game. Make a stock with the bones, water, carrots, and onion. Cut the fillets into long slices and put the rest of the meat through a grinder with an equal amount of pork.

Add a little of the game stock to the meats, along with 1 or 2 egg yolks, flour, salt, and pepper. Work in the Cognac and the Madeira.

Line a rectangular mold with *pâte pour pâté en croûte,* letting it overlap over the rims—the pâte should be about ⅛ inch thick. Fill the bottom with the meat mixture, line with the fillets, slices of liver, and of truffle. Spread over the rest of the meat.

Close up the pâté with another layer of pâte, moistening the edges to seal up all 4 sides well. Paint with egg yolk. Make a small chimney with a paper tunnel in the middle. Bake in a hot oven for 40 to 60 minutes depending on thickness.

Serve hot as it is or with *Sauce Périgueux* (page 261).

PÂTÉ DE GIBIER, VOLAILLE OU VEAU FROID, EN CROÛTE, À LA GELÉE

JELLIED GAME PÂTÉ

GAME
CHICKEN OR VEAL
PORK
WHITE WINE
COGNAC
MADEIRA
SALT
PEPPER
1 OR 2 EGG YOLKS
1 SPOON FLOUR
FRESH GOOSE OR
   DUCK LIVER
TRUFFLES
PÂTE POUR PÂTÉ EN
   CROÛTE (PAGE 82)
ASPIC JELLY
   (PAGE 267)

Take fillets off a few chickens and cut them into lengths (or the same with veal). Cut up the rest of the meats into big pieces (using the same quantity of pork as chicken) and leave to marinate overnight in a little white wine, Cognac, Madeira, salt, and pepper. Use the bones and trimmings to make a solid, gelatinous stock.

The next day make a hash of the meats (not too thin), add 1 or 2 egg yolks, the flour, the marinade, and mix well together to get a smooth, homogeneous mix.

Line a terrine mold—that is, one that dismantles—with *pâte pour pâté en croûte* of about ⅛ inch thick and letting it hang over the sides all around by a ½ inch. Half fill with the hash. Lay fillets across all the surface—with a slice of liver, a few slices of truffle the whole length—and finish by topping with the rest of the hash. Cover with a lid of *pâte pour pâté en croûte* or *pâte feuilletée* (page 58), seal up the edges, leaving a chimney in the middle with a rolled-up paper funnel. Paint with egg yolk, bake in a gentle oven for 2 hours.

Leave to cool and the next day pour into the paper funnel some almost-cold aspic jelly from the stock until almost full.

PÂTÉ DE CÈPES BEAUGENCY

BEAUGENCY MUSHROOM PÂTÉ

Porcini are especially fine mushrooms, but they can quickly become woody. If this happens, it can be enough to take off the stalk.

PORCINI
   MUSHROOMS
BUTTER
BAYONNE HAM
1 ONION
1 CLOVE GARLIC
2 SPOONS FLOUR
STOCK
PÂTE BRISÉE
   (PAGE 82)
1 EGG YOLK

Carefully wash some porcini, not too big and well closed. Take off the stalks and warm the heads through in butter for a few minutes.

Chop up the stalks and make a hash with a few slices of Bayonne ham, the onion, and garlic. Warm through in butter and sprinkle on the flour. Moisten with a little stock and allow to cook to get a consistent, even stuffing.

Line a tart mold with *pâte brisée*, about ⅛ inch thick, and leaving enough to cover the edges. Line the base with slices of Bayonne ham and then a layer of the mushroom hash. Arrange the porcini side by side, cover with another layer of the hash, and finish with more Bayonne ham. Close up the tart with another layer of pâte. Moisten the edges to seal it up well.

Paint with egg yolk. Make a little paper chimney in the center and bake in a medium oven for about 45 minutes.

Take out of its mold and serve very hot.

♈ Sancerre, white or red

QUICHE LORRAINE

QUICHE LORRAINE

You can replace the lardons and the ham with a layer of sliced Roquefort . . . or with thin slices of goose or duck liver and fresh truffle.

PÂTE BRISÉE
  (PAGE 82)
LARDONS
SMOKED HAM
BOILED HAM
BUTTER
EGGS
CREAM
PEPPER

Line a circular tart dish with a layer of unsweetened *pâte brisée*. Prick the bottom with a fork so the pastry does not rise. Sweat the lardons and ham in butter and lay on the pastry.

For 4 eggs, you need 2 cups of cream. Beat with a little pepper, as for an omelet, and pour over the ham. Bake in a hot oven for about 30 minutes. Serve very hot.

♎ Alsace, Champagne

PÂTÉ DE PÂQUES DU BERRY

EASTER PÂTÉ FROM BERRY

6 EGGS
PÂTE BRISÉE
  (PAGE 82)
1.5 LB SAUSAGE MEAT

Hard-boil the eggs.

Roll out a layer of *pâte brisée* into an oval ⅕ inch thick. Put half the uncooked sausage meat on the pastry leaving ¾ inch around the edges. Shell the eggs, slice lengthwise, and lay yolk-side down on the sausage meat. Cover with the rest of the sausage meat. Moisten the edges of the pastry.

Make a second sheet of pastry the same size as the first, but less thick. Cover the pâté and seal the edges. Paint with egg yolk and make a little chimney in the middle with a round of paper. Bake on a tray, in a medium oven, for 90 minutes. Serve hot or cold as a starter.

♎ Loire, red, or rosé

FROMAGE DE TÊTE DE PORC

PORK'S HEAD CHEESE

This inexpensive dish is popular as a starter, especially in winter.

HEAD OF PORK
BUTTER
SEA SALT
SALTPETER
ONIONS
CARROTS
LEEKS
CLOVES
THYME
BAY LEAF
PEPPERCORNS
GHERKINS
PARSLEY

Debone a fresh pig's head, not forgetting to take out the tongue and brain. Cook the brain in butter separately. Put the meat in a large dish to salt and leave for 48 hours, covered with sea salt and saltpeter.

Wash the head well in clean water a number of times. Place in a large marmite with onions, carrots, leeks, cloves, thyme, bay, peppercorns. Leave to cook slowly—just bubbling—for 2 hours.

Leave to cool. Take off all the fatty parts. Cut the meat into fat dice, except the tongue, which you cut in half lengthwise. Degrease the stock.

In a terrine, arrange a layer of diced meat, the cooked carrots, and the whole gherkins, and sprinkle with chopped parsley. Lay the tongue the length of the terrine. Finish by covering with the rest of the head meat. Fill the terrine with stock.

Chill before serving.

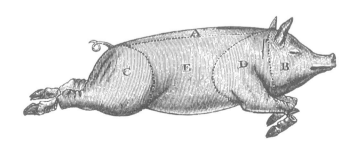

PÂTÉ DE FOIE DE CHEVREUIL

VENISON LIVER PÂTÉ

This pâté can be kept in jars that have been sterilized for 30 minutes. Then you always have hors d'œuvre on hand. Pork liver works in the same way.

2 LB VENISON LIVER
2 LB PORK NECK
BUTTER
2 SHALLOTS
SALT
PEPPER
COGNAC
2 GLASSES DRY WHITE
   WINE
2 EGGS
BACON

Trim the venison liver and put in a blender with the pork neck.

Warm through in butter the finely chopped shallots and mix in with the meats with salt, pepper, Cognac, dry white wine, and eggs. Mix everything to a smooth pâté.

Line the sides of an earthenware mold with the bacon. Fill up with the pâté and cover over with more bacon. Cover the terrine with a lid. Place in a bain-marie and cook in a moderate oven for 2 hours.

To check the cooking, slip a knitting needle into the middle—if it comes out clean, the pâté is cooked.

TERRINE AUX TROIS VIANDES

TERRINE OF PORK, VEAL, AND CHICKEN LIVER

3.5 LB SHOULDER
   OF PORK
3.25 LB VEAL BELLY
9 OZ CHICKEN LIVERS
½ ONION
2 SOUPSPOONS SALT
1 SOUPSPOON
   PEPPER
1 BOTTLE WHITE
   WINE

Separate out the fattier pieces of meat. Pick over any sinew from the pork or the veal. Chop the choicer bits into little dice. Mince the rest with the chicken livers and onion. Mix everything together with the salt and pepper, and add in the wine.

Pour the mixture into a terrine. Cook in a bain-marie in the oven, covered, for 60 to 70 minutes.

♀ Gewürztraminer, Riesling, Pouilly-Fuissé, or another dry white wine

(Opposite) Mère Brazier and Fernand Point in 1951

LES POISSONS
FISH

BOUILLABAISSE DE MARSEILLE

MARSEILLE BOUILLABAISSE

For a successful bouillabaisse, you must be able to appreciate the flavor of each fish. The stock is thickened only by boiling. Keep the plates warm and ready . . .

6.5 LB VERY FRESH
   FISH—RASCASSE
   (SCORPIONFISH),
   JOHN DORY,
   MONKFISH,
   WHITING
2 LOBSTERS
2 ONIONS
4 TOMATOES
4 CLOVES GARLIC
FENNEL LEAVES
2 BAY LEAVES
PINCH OF SAFFRON
SALT
PEPPERCORNS
SCANT CUP OLIVE OIL
SLICES OF BREAD
PARSLEY

Scale and gut the fish and wash in seawater if possible.

In a large, thick marmite—preferably cast iron—put roughly chopped onions, tomatoes, and garlic. Add a few leaves of fennel, the bay, saffron, salt, peppercorns, and olive oil. Mix everything together well.

Add the thick-fleshed fish first and, 5 minutes later, the rest— whiting, John Dory, lobster. Cover with boiling water. All the fish must be covered. Cook over a high heat for 15 minutes. The boil should be very hard—the quality of the dish depends on it. Leave it to bubble a few more minutes.

Cut some long slices of bread and let them dry in the oven without coloring. Put the bread in a soup tureen, and the fish in another bowl. Sieve the soup onto the bread and a little onto the fish. Sprinkle the bread with chopped parsley.

♀ White Hermitage

SOUPE DE POISSONS

FISH SOUP

This soup is a catch-all that makes use of the different fish in a market, bones and all.

4 OR 5 LEEKS
OLIVE OIL
TOMATOES
2 CLOVES GARLIC
PARSLEY
FENNEL LEAVES
1 CONGER EEL
ROCKFISH
CRABS (IF YOU
   HAVE THEM)
LOBSTER (OPTIONAL)
CROUTONS
1 PINCH SAFFRON
1 SPOON PASTIS
SALT
CAYENNE PEPPER
MUSSELS
BREAD
GRATED GRUYÈRE
   CHEESE

In a large casserole, warm through in olive oil the roughly chopped green part of the leeks. Add a few chopped tomatoes, the garlic, a few parsley stalks, some leaves of fennel, and moisten—pour over 5 quarts of water. Bring to a boil.

Add the head and bones of the eel and then all the small rockfish you can find. You can also put in 2 pounds of small crabs and a lobster, which you take out after 15 minutes cooking. Leave to simmer for 4 to 5 hours and then strain.

Leave over heat to reduce to get a smooth consommé. Finish with a seasoning of saffron, pastis, salt, cayenne pepper, and a few mussels strewn in the soup dish as garnish.

Prepare some small croutons from the bread, lightly colored in the oven and rubbed on one side with garlic. Serve on very hot plates—the croutons separately at the table—and as much grated cheese as you like.

♟ Rosé de Provence

GRATIN DE FRUITS DE MER

SHELLFISH GRATIN

The shrimp family is vast and comprises more than 160 species. The crevettes roses *and* grises *are the most widely found in Europe.*

MUSHROOMS
BUTTER
4 SCALLOPS (ANY
  SHELLFISH CAN
  BE USED)
MUSSELS
4 SOLE FILLETS
2 OZ SHRIMP
1 GLASS DRY WHITE
  WINE
SALT
PEPPER
BEURRE MANIÉ
  (PAGE 254)
2 TO 3 SPOONS
  HEAVY CREAM
1 GLASS COGNAC
GRATED CHEESE
FLOUR

Sweat some mushrooms in butter.

Open all the scallops, mussels, and any other shellfish with a knife or in the oven. Take out the flesh. Cut the fillets of sole in two. Clean everything and put on to cook slowly in a frying pan with the shrimp and the white wine, salt, and pepper. The cooking lasts about 10 minutes. Lift the shrimp out and take off the shells.

Pour the cooking liquid into a new pan. Bind the sauce with the *beurre manié*, adding in the heavy cream.

Flambé the fish in warm Cognac and place in a gratin dish with the mushrooms. Top with the sauce. Cover the surface with grated cheese and gratinate in a hot oven.

♀ Riesling, Sylvaner

ÉCREVISSES À LA NAGE

CRAYFISH IN THEIR JUS

CARROTS
ONIONS
SHALLOTS
PARSLEY
SALT
PEPPERCORNS
DRY WHITE WINE
10 FINE CRAYFISH
  PER PERSON

Cut up the carrots, onions, and shallots. Cook them in enough water to half cover the crayfish. When the vegetables are cooked, add the parsley, salt, and peppercorns. Allow to boil for 10 minutes, then add the dry white wine.

Bring back to a boil and throw in the cleaned crayfish. Cook for 10 minutes.

Serve in their cooking liquid.

♀ White Mâcon, Muscadet

LA MÈRE'S
CLASSIC MENU NO.3

Terrine Maison

House Pâté

◆

Langouste Mayonnaise

Lobster with Mayonnaise (page 97)

◆

Poulet à la Crème aux Morilles

Chicken with Morels and Cream

(page 145)

◆

Fromages de Saison

Seasonal Cheeses

◆

Pêches Glacées Flambées au Kirsch

Peaches Flamed with Kirsch (page 249)

ÉCREVISSES À LA BORDELAISE

CRAYFISH BORDELAISE

Crayfish should always be gutted—that is to say, lift out their intestines before preparing—otherwise they can have a bitter flavor.

100 CRAYFISH
1 QUART MILK
2½ CUPS BUTTER
4 CARROTS
3 LARGE ONIONS
PARSLEY
TARRAGON
SALT
PEPPER
THYME
BAY LEAF
1 GLASS COGNAC
1 BOTTLE DRY WHITE
   WINE
1 GLASS FISH FUMET
7 OZ TOMATO PUREE
CAYENNE PEPPER

Clean the crayfish and put in the milk to soak for 1 hour.

In a frying pan, put ½ cup of butter with a hash made up of the carrots, onions, parsley stalks, and tarragon. Add salt, pepper, thyme, and bay.

Drain the crayfish, lift off the black veins and intestines, and throw into the saucepan. Sprinkle with a pinch of pepper. Leave to cook until the crayfish turn a good red. Flambé with warm Cognac.

Take the crayfish out of the pan and keep warm. Pour the white wine into the pan. Reduce it by half.

Put the crayfish back. Add in the fish fumet, tomato puree, and cook for 10 minutes. Lay up the crayfish in a large hot bowl. Sieve the sauce into a new casserole. Start to reduce it and then build it up again by adding little pieces of butter, one at a time, and whisking very hard. Pour the sauce over the crayfish. Sprinkle with chopped parsley and cayenne pepper.

♉ Sancerre, Muscadet

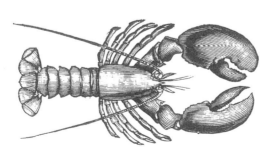

GRATIN DE QUEUES D'ÉCREVISSE

GRATIN OF CRAYFISH TAILS

6.5 LB CRAYFISH
COURT BOUILLON
BUTTER
MUSHROOMS
TRUFFLE
SAUCE BÉCHAMEL
    (PAGE 255)
1 DESSERTSPOON
    BEURRE
    D'ÉCREVISSE
    (PAGE 253)
CREAM
SALT
PEPPER

Wash the crayfish and lift out the black vein and intestines down the tail. Cook for 10 minutes in a little court bouillon. Leave to cool.

Take the meat out of the shells—body and claws—keeping all the shells. Sweat the meat in a small frying pan with a little butter, a few mushrooms, and chopped truffle.

Make a béchamel, half and half with milk and cream. Salt, pepper, and leave to cook for a few minutes.

Mix the crayfish, truffle, and mushrooms into the béchamel, and add the crayfish butter. Pour into a gratin dish and finish at the top of a hot oven.

♀ Pouilly-Fuissé, white Hermitage

LANGOUSTE MAYONNAISE

LOBSTER WITH MAYONNAISE

PARSLEY
PEPPERCORNS
CARROTS
ONION
CLOVES
GARLIC
LEMON ZEST
THYME
BAY LEAF
CHERVIL
TARRAGON
VINEGAR
1 (1.5-LB) LIVE
    LOBSTER
SAUCE MAYONNAISE
    (PAGE 259)

Make a court bouillon: Bring some cold water to a boil with parsley, peppercorns, carrot, an onion stuck with cloves, garlic, lemon zest, thyme, bay, chervil, and tarragon. Let it bubble gently for 30 minutes.

Add the vinegar, bring back to a boil and plunge in the bound lobster. Allow 15 to 20 minutes cooking time.

While the lobster is warm, serve it up—cut in two—on lettuce leaves. Accompany with the *sauce mayonnaise*.

LANGOUSTE BELLE AURORE

LOBSTER WITH BRANDY AND CREAM

If you are short on lobster, it is possible to serve this inside a pastry case—like a vol au vent—with a boiling sauce to the side.

1 CARROT
2 SHALLOTS
OLIVE OIL
1 (2.25-LB) LIVE
LOBSTER
1 GLASS COGNAC
SALT
PEPPER
SAFFRON
BEURRE MANIÉ
(PAGE 254)
4¼ CUPS HEAVY
CREAM

Make up a mirepoix of vegetables—mostly diced carrot and shallot—in a deep saucepan with a little olive oil. Put the live lobster in, cut in half, head to one side, tail to the other. Let it cook for a few minutes, add the Cognac, and flambé.

Dampen with enough water to half cover. Season with salt, pepper, and a pinch of saffron. Cook, covered, for 30 minutes.

Take out the lobster and reduce the liquid until there are just 2 cups of sauce left.

While the sauce is reducing, take the meat out of the lobster— the edible parts from the head and claws. Cut the tail into medallions. Put all the meat in a gratin dish.

Sieve the sauce reduction through muslin into a small casserole. Bind it with a small amount of *beurre manié*. Add the cream, and bring to a boil. Taste and adjust the seasoning as you like. This sauce should be quite mild so as not to soften the flavor of the lobster—don't abuse the pepper or the Cognac.

Pour the sauce over the lobster. Put in the oven for 10 to 15 minutes.

♉ Brut Champagne, white Burgundy, white Hermitage, preferably Chante-Alouette from Chapoutier

GRATIN DE LANGOUSTE CATHERINE

GRATIN OF LOBSTER CATHERINE

CARROT
SHALLOT
OLIVE OIL
1 (1.25-LB) LOBSTER
2 GLASSES COGNAC
SALT
PEPPER
1 PINCH SAFFRON
BUTTER
MUSHROOMS
SAUCE AMÉRICAINE
HEAVY CREAM

Make a mirepoix of roughly chopped carrot and shallot in a thick-bottomed frying pan with a little olive oil. Put the lobster in, cut in half with head to one side, tail to the other. Leave to color a few minutes. Warm 1 glass of Cognac, pour over the lobster, and flambé.

Half cover with water. Season with salt, pepper, and saffron. Cook, covered, for about 30 minutes.

Butter a gratin dish and cover with a layer of finely sliced mushrooms. Slip the lobster out of its shell. Slice the tail into medallions. Arrange the medallions down the middle of the gratin dish and surround with the meat from the lobster claws and head. Baste with a glass of Cognac. Add to the *Sauce Américaine* a few spoons of heavy cream, and pour over the lobster. Put in the top of a very hot oven.

Serve with Creole rice.

♟ Pouilly-Fumé, Pouilly-Fuissé

LANGOUSTE AU RICARD

LOBSTER WITH RICARD

1 (1.75-LB) LOBSTER
SALT
PEPPER
5 TABLESPOONS
   RICARD
BEURRE D'ESCARGOTS
   (PAGE 253)
1 EGG YOLK
1 TABLESPOON HEAVY
   CREAM

Split the lobster in half lengthwise. Set the 2 sides in a long earthenware dish. Salt, pepper, and baste with 4 tablespoons of the Ricard. Cook in a very hot oven for 7 minutes.

Take out of the oven. Have ready the *beurre d'escargots*, mixed with an egg yolk, the heavy cream, and the last tablespoon of Ricard. Spread this mix on both sides of the lobster. Put it back in the oven for 12 minutes.

Serve in the baking dish.

♟ Provence white

HOMARD DU GRAND MAÎTRE

LOBSTER GRAND MAÎTRE

The Brittany lobster, midnight-blue in color, is the best of all, especially in summer.

- ½ CUP BUTTER
- ½ CUP OIL
- CARROTS
- SHALLOTS
- PARSLEY
- 2 (1.25-LB) LOBSTERS
- 2½ CUPS BELGIAN BEER
- SALT
- PEPPER
- 2 EGG YOLKS
- 3 SPOONS HEAVY CREAM

In a frying pan with a thick bottom, warm the butter and oil. Make a mirepoix, chopping up the carrots, shallots, and parsley stalks finely. Add to the pan. Chop up the live lobsters and throw into the frying pan. Let them stiffen for a few minutes.

Add the beer, salt (very little), and pepper, and leave to cook, covered, for 15 minutes.

Take out the pieces of lobster, take the meat out of the shell, and keep the meat warm. Reduce the cooking liquid by half.

Leave the sauce to cool a little and bind with beaten egg yolks and the heavy cream. Adjust the seasoning. Sieve the sauce over the lobster on the plate.

Serve with Creole rice.

🍷 Gewürztraminer, Riesling

LANGOUSTE GRILLÉE AU CURRY

BROILED LOBSTER CURRY

You can accompany this lobster with a lemony Sauce Hollandaise *(page 257).*

- 1 (1.75-LB) LOBSTER
- PEPPER
- CURRY POWDER
- OLIVE OIL
- SALT

Split the live lobster in half lengthwise. Pepper and sprinkle on a pinch of curry powder.

Baste well with olive oil. Place under a broiler and turn the heat right up. Cook for 20 minutes, basting often with the oil and juices caught under the broiler.

Serve the lobster with pilaf rice seasoned with a teaspoon of curry powder in the cooking.

🍷 Pouilly-Fuissé, Muscadet

LANGOUSTE À L'AMÉRICAINE

LOBSTER AMÉRICAINE

This method is the same for lobsters or crayfish.

SHALLOTS
CARROTS
OLIVE OIL
1 (1.75-LB) LOBSTER
1 GLASS COGNAC
½ BOTTLE DRY WHITE
 WINE
PEPPER
CAYENNE PEPPER
TOMATO PUREE
BEURRE MANIÉ
 (PAGE 254)
BUTTER
PARSLEY

In a frying pan big enough to hold the lobster, prepare a mirepoix of chopped carrots and shallots, warmed through in olive oil.

Wash and clean the lobster and cut up while still alive—the tail in medallions of 1¼ inches thick. Split the head in half lengthwise. It is necessary to work very quickly so the lobster does not suffer. Put the pieces in the frying pan and cook quickly to get a good red color.

Warm the Cognac, pour over the lobster, and flambé. Moisten with the dry white wine. Pepper, add a pinch of cayenne and a spoon of tomato puree. Cover and cook slowly for 15 to 20 minutes.

Take out the lobster and remove the meat from the shell—head and body. Keep them warm. Reduce the cooking liquid by half and sieve into a casserole. Bind with the *beurre manié* and check the seasoning, which should be distinct but not so much that it masks that natural flavor of the lobster.

Present the lobster on a plate. Take the sauce off the heat, whisk in a good piece of butter vigorously.

Pour over the lobster and garnish with chopped parsley. Serve quickly.

Always serve on very hot plates.

♗ Chablis, Meursault, Montrachet

LANGOUSTE À LA CARDINAL

LOBSTER CARDINAL

In a lobster, we only eat the tail, but even so the carcass can be used to prepare soups and sauces.

OLIVE OIL
CARROTS
ONIONS
CELERY
PARSLEY
TOMATOES
1 CLOVE GARLIC
TARRAGON
1 (1.75-LB) LOBSTER
1 GLASS COGNAC
1 BOTTLE DRY WHITE
  WINE
BOUQUET GARNI
SALT
PEPPER
1 GOOD SOLE
2 TO 3 SPOONS
  THICK HEAVY
  CREAM

Make a mirepoix, dicing carrots, onions, celery, and parsley. Cook in oil in a frying pan.

Add a few tomatoes, chopped in quarters, garlic, tarragon (very little). Put the lobster in alive. Baste with warm Cognac and flambé.

Add the dry white wine, bouquet garni, very little salt, pepper, and leave to cook, covered, for 30 minutes.

Trim and skin the sole. Take out the lobster and replace it with the sole. Let it poach until cooked. Take out and lift the fillets off the bone. Reduce the sauce by half. Add the heavy cream.

Take the tail meat out of the lobster. Cut into medallions.

Put in a copper casserole, as per tradition, the 4 fillets of sole. Place on top the medallions of lobster. Sieve the sauce over them—careful, this sauce should be quite clear and not have any bits in it.

Serve with pilaf rice.

♀ Meursault, Chablis

(Opposite) Eugénie Brazier and Gaston, her son

COQUILLES SAINT-JACQUES AU GRATIN

GRATIN OF SCALLOPS

12 SCALLOPS
COURT BOUILLON
ONION
GARLIC
MUSHROOMS
BUTTER
2 SHALLOTS
PARSLEY
ROUX BLOND
    (PAGE 263)
1 GLASS DRY WHITE
    WINE
1 EGG YOLK
BREAD CRUMBS
SALT
PEPPER

Open the scallop shells in the oven or in a frying pan. Take out the scallop and corals and throw away the rest.

Wash the shells and the scallops. Simmer the scallops in a court bouillon with onion and garlic for about 10 minutes. Slice and sweat some mushrooms in butter.

Chop the scallop meats and corals with the shallots, parsley, and the mushrooms.

Make the *roux blond*, warming gently. Add the wine and a little of the court bouillon, but the sauce should still be quite thick. Bind with an egg yolk.

Bind the chopped scallops and shallots with the sauce, and put back in the shell. Adjust the seasoning with salt and pepper. Cover with bread crumbs. Put a good piece of butter on each scallop and brown in a hot oven for 10 minutes.

♀ White Mâcon, white Hermitage

COQUILLES SAINT-JACQUES AU CHAMPAGNE

SCALLOPS IN CHAMPAGNE

12 SCALLOPS
BUTTER
4 OZ MUSHROOMS
SHALLOTS
½ BOTTLE
  CHAMPAGNE
3 SPOONS HEAVY
  CREAM
SALT
PEPPER
BEURRE MANIÉ
  (PAGE 254)
1 EGG YOLK

Lift the scallops and their corals out of the shells. Warm some butter in a frying pan and slowly color some diced shallots and sliced mushrooms. Add the scallops. Wash the pan in the Champagne and heavy cream. Cook without boiling, stirring regularly, for 10 minutes. Salt and pepper.

Lift the scallops out and reduce the sauce by half. Bind with the *beurre manié*, to which you add an egg yolk—away from the flame.

Put the scallops and the sauce together in a gratin dish. Brown under the broiler.

♀ White Mâcon, Pouilly-Fuissé

MOUCLADE DE L'AUNIS

MUSSELS IN CREAM AND SAFFRON

8.5 LB MUSSELS
BUTTER
3 SHALLOTS
6 TABLESPOONS HEAVY CREAM
1 PINCH SAFFRON
2 EGG YOLKS
PEPPER
PARSLEY

Rope-grown mussels (mussels that are grown on and harvested from ropes) are often just as good as wild mussels from Holland.

Carefully clean the mussels. Do not put the mussels in water or they will open. Open them raw, so the meat stays in a single half-shell.

Warm finely chopped shallots through in butter—preferably in a frying pan. Add the heavy cream, saffron, and bind with the egg yolks, away from the flame. Pepper. Put back on the heat and throw the mussels (in their shells) into this boiling sauce. Leave to cook for 5 minutes. Serve in the cooking dish, sprinkled with chopped parsley.

Be sure the guests' plates are warm.

🍷 White Mâcon, Muscadet

MOULES SAUCE POULETTE

MUSSELS POULETTE

7 LB MUSSELS
2 SHALLOTS
PEPPER
PARSLEY
2 GLASSES DRY WHITE WINE
BEURRE MANIÉ (PAGE 254)
HEAVY CREAM
2 EGG YOLKS
BUTTER
LEMON JUICE

Put the mussels in a saucepan big enough that they can be easily shaken up. Add finely chopped shallots, pepper, chopped parsley, and dry white wine. Cover and cook over a high flame until all the mussels have opened. Give them a good shake to make sure they are open.

Pour the sauce off into a new pan, being careful not to go all the way to the bottom in case there is any sand. Bind the cooking liquor with the *beurre manié*. Add a few spoons of heavy cream and, away from the flame, the egg yolks—whipping vigorously—then a piece of fresh butter. Adjust the seasoning and add, according to your taste, some lemon juice.

Take one half of the shell off each mussel and pour over the sauce. Serve in hot bowls.

🍷 Muscadet, Sancerre

MOULES AU RIZ PILAF

MUSSEL PILAF

3.5 LB ROPE-GROWN
   MUSSELS
2 SPOONS OLIVE OIL
2 SHALLOTS
RICE
THYME
½ BAY LEAF
2 TO 3 CLOVES
1 CLOVE GARLIC
PEPPER
SALT

Scrub the mussels clean, lifting off any beard.

In a frying pan, open the mussels over a high flame. Keep the cooking liquid, emptying the pan carefully to be sure not to get any grains of sand from the bottom. Take the mussels out of their shells and keep warm.

In the olive oil, warm finely chopped shallots in a new frying pan. Add the rice. Stir well without letting the rice color. Cover the rice with two-and-a-half times its volume of the cooking liquor from the mussels, extended with stock or water. Add the thyme, bay, cloves, garlic, a few grinds of pepper, and salt if needed. Cover and cook in the oven for 17 minutes.

When the rice is cooked, mix the mussels in carefully.

Serve very hot from the cooking pan. Check that the plates are hot.

♀ White, young, fresh rosé

MOULES MARINIÈRE

MUSSELS IN WHITE WINE AND SHALLOTS

7 LB MUSSELS
PEPPER
PARSLEY
THYME
SHALLOTS
2 GLASSES DRY
   WHITE WINE
BUTTER

Scrub the mussels clean.

Put them in a large enough pan to be able to give them a good shake later. Add pepper (no salt), parsley, thyme, chopped shallots, and dry white wine. Cook over a lively flame, covered, until all the mussels have opened. Check them by giving them a few good shakes of the pan.

Pour off the cooking liquid into a new pan—without going all the way to the bottom, as there may be some grains of sand left. Reduce by half. Add in some chopped parsley and, at the last moment, a big piece of butter. Serve the mussels still in their shells with the sauce.

♀ Sancerre, Muscadet

DARNES DE SAUMON BONNE FEMME

SALMON BONNE FEMME

1 (5-OZ) SALMON
   STEAK PER PERSON
BUTTER
2 SHALLOTS
MUSHROOMS
SALT
PEPPER
DRY WHITE WINE
SAUCE HOLLANDAISE
   (PAGE 257)

Scale and gut the salmon. Wash and pat dry. Cut into steaks of around 1 inch thick. Put them in a well-buttered gratin dish, add finely chopped shallots, diced raw mushrooms; salt, pepper. Add in enough white wine to go up ¾ inch from the bottom of the dish.

Cover with greased baking paper and cook slowly in a medium oven. We judge the fish is cooked when the central bone comes away easily.

Take out of the oven and put the cooking liquid in a thick-bottomed saucepan. Reduce by three-quarters.

Mix the reduction with an equal quantity of *sauce hollandaise*. Pour over each steak. Pass under a broiler—a few seconds should be enough to color the surface. Be careful not to burn it.

♉ Chablis, Meursault

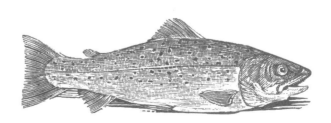

CHAUDRÉE CHARENTAISE

CHARENTE SEAFOOD CASSEROLE

4 OR 5 SQUID
2 SOLES
2 SMALL SKATE
CONGER EEL
15 CLOVES GARLIC
BOUQUET GARNI
SALT
PEPPER
DRY WHITE WINE
¾ CUP BEURRE DE
   CHARENTE

Skate has no bones and its main cartilage comes off without a problem, which makes it easy to cook.

Start by cleaning the squid and put them on to cook in salted water.

Prepare the skate, soles, and eel, and cook separately—cook the soles and the skate until both skins can be lifted off the sole, and the cartilage can be lifted off the skate.

Put all the fish pieces in the bottom of a marmite with peeled garlic cloves, bouquet garni (thyme, bay, parsley), salt, and pepper. Cover with white wine. Cover and put over the heat. At the moment it starts to simmer, add in the almost-cooked squid. Cook for 30 minutes.

Serve in a large dish and add in, at the last moment, the Charente butter.

♆ Muscadet, Sancerre

SOLE GRILLÉE

BROILED SOLE

Coldwater sole are best. Equally, sole fished in deep waters are better than those from inshore. You should always choose a very fresh and fat fish.

1 (14-OZ) SOLE
SALT
PEPPER
OLIVE OIL
PARSLEY
1 LEMON
BUTTER

Take both skins off the sole. Salt, pepper, and pour on some olive oil. Broil or—better still—grill on a barbecue. Take the fish out just as it has cooked—the fillets will start to come away from the bone. Heat a small poker to red and mark the fish with a crisscross. Scatter over a little chopped parsley.

Serve with the 4 lemon quarters, fresh butter, and some steamed potatoes.

♈ This year's Mâcon

FILETS DE SOLE SAINT-GERMAIN

SOLE ST. GERMAIN

1 (14-OZ) SOLE
SALT
PEPPER
BUTTER
BREAD CRUMBS
PARSLEY
SAUCE BÉARNAISE
   (PAGE 255)

Take the fillets off the sole; salt, pepper. Paint with melted butter and sprinkle with the bread crumbs. Baste with the melted butter and broil slowly.

Put on each fillet a soupspoon of *sauce béarnaise* and a little chopped parsley. Serve on a plate surrounded by sautéed new potatoes.

♈ Pouilly-Fuissé, white Mâcon

CAPRICE DE FILETS DE SOLE

SOLE CAPRICE

1 (14-OZ) SOLE
SALT
PEPPER
1 CARROT
TRUFFLE SHAVINGS
BUTTER
1 GLASS MADEIRA
BEURRE MANIÉ
   (PAGE 254)
3 SOUPSPOONS
   HEAVY CREAM
CAYENNE PEPPER
2 TOMATOES
MUSHROOMS
PARSLEY

Lift the 4 fillets off the sole. Add salt and a pinch of pepper. Fold the fillets back on themselves and put them in a gratin dish.

In a casserole, steam the diced carrot and a truffle skin or shavings. Leave to bubble, covered, for 5 minutes, with a good piece of butter. Add in a good glass of Madeira and leave to bubble again for 3 minutes.

Pour this sauce over the sole fillets. Put them in the oven for about 10 minutes.

Take out of the oven, pour off the sauce into a new pan, and reduce. Bind with the *beurre manié* and add the heavy cream. Adjust the seasoning. Add the cayenne pepper.

On each fillet, place half a tomato, peeled, seeded, and sautéed in butter. In the tomato put some mushrooms sautéed in butter and scatter with fresh parsley.

Pour the sauce over the fillets without sieving.

♀ White Arbois, Sancerre

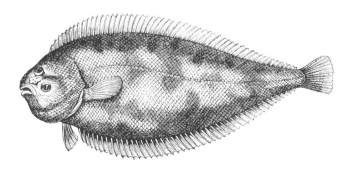

FILETS DE SOLE À LA NORMANDE

SOLE NORMANDY

You can decorate the plate with flowers, leaves, slices of truffle, trussed crayfish, or breaded strips of chicken or fish as you like . . .

2 (14-OZ) SOLES
MUSSELS
MUSHROOMS
LEMON
BUTTER
BEURRE MANIÉ
    (PAGE 254)
HEAVY CREAM
1 EGG YOLK
SALT
PEPPER
COOKED SHRIMP

Take the heads off the soles, the black skin, and gut them. Steam open the mussels, take out the flesh, and keep warm. Keep the cooking liquor. Slice the mushrooms and cook in a little well-salted water with a squirt of lemon.

Butter up a gratin dish. Put the fillets in with the cooking liquor from the mussels and the mushrooms. Cover with parchment and cook in a medium oven until the fillets start to come away easily. Remove the bones and the white skin of the soles. Keep the fillets warm and covered.

Reduce the cooking liquid and bind with the *beure manié*. Add a few tablespoons of heavy cream. Bring to a boil then take off the heat and whisk in an egg yolk. Check the seasoning.

Arrange the sole fillets in the middle of the plate, surrounded by the mussels, shelled shrimp, and mushrooms. Put back in the oven for a few moments and then pour on the sauce.

♇ Muscadet, Sancerre

FILETS DE SOLE À LA BOURGUIGNONNE

SOLE BURGUNDY

1 (14-OZ) SOLE
BUTTER
3 SHALLOTS
3.5 OZ MUSHROOMS
SALT
PEPPER
2 GLASSES
  BEAUJOLAIS
BEURRE MANIÉ
  (PAGE 254)
PARSLEY

Take the fillets off the sole. Butter a gratin dish and lay the fillets in, with chopped shallots and diced mushrooms. Salt and give a grind of pepper. Add 2 good glasses of Beaujolais. Cook in a hot oven for about 10 minutes.

Take out of the oven and pour the liquids into a pan. Reduce by half, then bind with the *beurre manié*. At the last minute, add a good nut of butter and pour the sauce over the sole. Scatter over chopped parsley.

♓ White Mâcon

SOLE LUCIE

SOLE IN CHAMPAGNE

1 (14-OZ) SOLE
BUTTER
SHALLOTS
SALT
PEPPER
2 GLASSES BRUT
  CHAMPAGNE
MUSHROOMS
TRUFFLES
BEURRE MANIÉ
  (PAGE 254)

Trim the sole, lift off the 2 skins and gut the fish.

Butter a large gratin dish well and line the bottom with finely chopped shallot. Put the sole in, salt, pepper, and baste with the brut Champagne. Cook in a hot oven for 15 minutes.

Take the sole out, lift off the fillets, and remove all the bones. Pour the cooking liquor into a new pan and reduce.

Slice some mushrooms and cook in butter. Re-form the sole by filling the insides with the mushrooms and slices of truffle. Lightly bind the sauce with the *beurre manié*. Pour the sauce over the sole and slide under the broiler to lightly brown.

♓ Pouilly-Fuissé, Pouilly-Fumé

FILETS DE SOLE GALLIENI

SOLE GALLIENI

Joseph Gallieni was a French marshal, credited with masterminding victory in the First Battle of the Marne in 1914.

1 (1.5-LB) SOLE
4 OR 5 MUSHROOMS
1 GLASS DRY WHITE
  WINE
BUTTER
SALT
PEPPER
BREAD CRUMBS
10 LEAVES SORREL
SCANT CUP HEAVY
  CREAM
½ LEMON

Take the fillets off the sole. Trim and flatten lightly. Make a little stock with the bones, head, mushroom stalks, and white wine.

Melt some butter gently in a long gratin dish and add the salt and the pepper. Dredge the sole through bread crumbs—on one side only. Add to the pan (crumb side up) and cook in hot oven for 10 minutes, under the broiler preferably, basting often with the butter.

Make a sauce with the sorrel—stalks removed, finely chopped— and chopped mushrooms. Put everything in a small pan with a good nut of butter. Cover and let cook over a good flame for 7 to 8 minutes. Add ½ cup of the fish stock and the heavy cream. Leave to reduce some more. Add the juice of half a lemon and a nut of butter, away from the heat.

Pour half this sauce over the golden sole and serve the rest on the side in a sauceboat. Be sure the plates are very hot.

♀ White Châteauneuf-du-Pape

SOLE HERMITAGE

SOLE HERMITAGE

1 (14-OZ) SOLE
¾ CUP BUTTER
1 SHALLOT
CHIVES
PARSLEY
1 OZ BREAD
2 EGG YOLKS
2 GLASSES DRY WHITE
  WINE
SALT
PEPPER

Clean the sole and lift off the 2 skins—black and white. Make a cut into the bone, as if filleting, but go no more than 1 ½ inches deep inside.

Into this opening, slide the following mixture: the butter, softened and mixed with chopped shallot, chives, and parsley; the bread and the egg yolks; salt; and pepper.

In a well-buttered gratin dish, place the stuffed sole and pour over 2 good glasses of dry white wine. Cook in a hot oven for 15 minutes. Serve in its cooking dish.

☿ White Hermitage

SOLE MEUNIÈRE AUX CÈPES

SOLE WITH PORCINI MUSHROOMS

1 (14-OZ) SOLE
SALT
PEPPER
FLOUR
BUTTER
FRESH PORCINI
  MUSHROOMS
PARSLEY

Take the black skin off the sole, then trim and gut it; rinse and dry. Salt, pepper, and dredge in some flour, then tap to knock off any excess. Fry in a cast-iron pan in a big piece of very hot butter. After a few minutes, turn the fish over. After this first, quick cooking, put in the oven.

Slice and sauté the porcini in butter.

When the fillets start to come away from the bone, the sole is cooked. Slide onto a long plate into which you have poured some melted butter. Pour the mushrooms on top. Scatter with chopped parsley.

☿ Pouilly-Fuissé, Pouilly-Fumé

TURBOT AU CHAMBERTIN

TURBOT COOKED IN CHAMBERTIN

If you do not have Chambertin, you can use a good, young, rough Burgundy. Turbot is a delicious fish, but there is a lot of waste. Allowing for taking out the fillets, you'll need around one pound of untrimmed fish per person. Choose a thick fish.

4.5 LB TURBOT
1 CUP BUTTER
2 TO 3 SHALLOTS
SALT
PEPPER
1 BOTTLE
  CHAMBERTIN
BEURRE MANIÉ
  (PAGE 254)
PARSLEY

Take off the fillets from the turbot. Put them in a large, ovenproof dish. Add the white skin from the belly and a few bones cut large. Add in a good piece of butter, 2 or 3 whole shallots, salt—very little—pepper.

Cover with the Chambertin. Cover with greaseproof paper. Place in a medium oven. When the liquid boils, take the dish out of the oven, drain the fillets, and cut into fat steaks—1 per person. Keep warm.

Reduce the cooking liquid until there is just enough sauce. Sieve it. Bind with the *beurre manié*, check that the seasoning is pronounced, and bring back to a boil.

At the last minute, and away from the flame, add in a good piece of fresh butter and whisk vigorously. Pour over the turbot fillets. Sprinkle over some chopped parsley.

This can be served with croutons fried with garlic in a pan, but watch out for the garlic if the meal is to be followed by an evening's dancing . . .

♈ Chambertin, Burgundy, or white Château-Chalon

TURBOT GRILLÉ
À LA HOLLANDAISE

BROILED TURBOT WITH HOLLANDAISE

This dish seems simple, but needs long cooking because turbot can be very thick. You need a big oven or barbecue.

14 OZ UNCUT TURBOT
   PER PERSON
HERBES DE PROVENCE
OLIVE OIL
SALT
PEPPER
SAUCE HOLLANDAISE
   (OPTIONAL,
   PAGE 257)
SALTED BUTTER
LEMON
PARSLEY

Wash the turbot, gut, and stuff with herbes de Provence. Paint well with olive oil. Salt, pepper, and scatter more herbs outside.

Place under a broiler or over a charcoal grill. We count 90 minutes for each side, turning often—the time depending on the size of the fish.

Serve with *sauce hollandaise* with plenty of lemon, or simply with fresh butter, salt, lemon, and parsley. Serve with steamed potatoes.

♀ Very dry new Mâcon, fruity Muscadet

FILETS DE TURBOTIN LÉA

FILLETS OF SMALL TURBOT LEA

It is easy to fillet a fish if you wipe your knife through fine salt regularly.

1 YOUNG TURBOT
BUTTER
1 SHALLOT
SALT
PEPPER
DRY WHITE WINE
TOMATO
MUSHROOMS
HEAVY CREAM
BREAD CRUMBS

Take the fillets off a fine young turbot. Place them in a well-buttered gratin dish. Scatter over a finely chopped shallot, salt, and pepper. Fill up to half-full with dry white wine.

Peel and seed some tomatoes. Chop them roughly and let them reduce in butter to get a puree. Spread on each fillet. Mix into this puree a few finely chopped raw mushrooms.

Sauce each fillet with a spoon of heavy cream. Sprinkle with bread crumbs and cook in a hot oven for about 15 minutes, depending on the thickness of the fillets.

Serve from the baking dish as it comes out of the oven.

♀ Pouilly-Fuissé, Chablis

ROUGETS EN PAPILLOTES

RED MULLET IN PACKETS

1 (7-OZ) RED MULLET
  PER PERSON
OLIVE OIL
BAY LEAVES
BACON
PEPPER
BUTTER
LEMON
PARSLEY

Scale and clean the red mullets without gutting them. Place each fish on a sheet of aluminum foil, generously oiled with olive oil. On one side of each fish put a bay leaf; on the other a thin slice of bacon. Pepper lightly and wrap the foil into a parcel. Cook gently under a broiler, or on a barbecue, for 15 to 20 minutes.

Open the parcels on the plates. Serve with a parsley and lemon butter or, for a more sophisticated touch, with *Sauce Hollandaise* (page 257), seasoned with a little anchovy puree.

♟ Dry white, rosé de Provence

ROUGETS À LA NIÇOISE

RED MULLET NICOISE

1 GOOD-SIZED RED
  MULLET PER PERSON
OIL
TOMATOES
GARLIC
TARRAGON
ANCHOVY FILLETS
LEMON
PARSLEY
BLACK OLIVES

Scale, trim, wash, and drain the red mullets. Put some oil in a saucepan and warm the mullets through.

Place the fish in a gratin dish, cover with a fresh tomato puree mixed with crushed garlic and chopped tarragon. Cook in the oven for 15 to 20 minutes.

Let cool. Arrange on a long plate with a few anchovy fillets on each mullet and rounds of lemon. Sprinkle with chopped parsley. Garnish the plate with black olives. Serve cold.

♟ Rosé du Var

ROUGETS MONTE-CARLO

RED MULLET MONTE CARLO

Fun and easy to make outdoors.

2 SMALL RED MULLETS
PER PERSON
OLIVE OIL
SALT
PEPPER
BREAD
BUTTER
ANCHOVY PUREE
BEURRE D'ANCHOIS
(PAGE 252)
LEMON

Scale the red mullets, gut, wash, and dry. With a sharp knife, make angled incisions on both sides. Wipe with olive oil; salt and pepper. Grill on the barbecue, preferably over wood.

Slice some bread and fry gently in butter, then cover with anchovy puree. Put a red mullet on each crouton and serve with *beurre d'anchois*, straw potatoes, and quarters of lemon.

♀ Rosé de Provence

GRONDIN FARCI TRUFFÉ À LA BOULONNAISE

GURNET STUFFED WITH TRUFFLES

Gurnets are round, quite bony fish. If they are not readily available, you can use either a small codling or a sea bream as a substitute.

1 (6.5-LB) GURNET
1 LB PORK SAUSAGE
MEAT
WHITE BREAD
1 LARGE ONION
1 CLOVE GARLIC
1 HANDFUL PARSLEY
2 EGGS
1 GLASS COGNAC
1 BOTTLE DRY WHITE
WINE
TRUFFLE SHAVINGS
SALT
PEPPER
BUTTER

Trim, scale, gut, and clean the fish. Split it down the back to lift out the bone.

Knead the sausage meat together with the white of the bread, chopped onion, garlic, and parsley, the eggs, and Cognac. Fry this mix for a few minutes and add in a glass of white wine. Leave to cool, then add the truffle shavings, salt, and pepper.

Stuff the gurnet and stitch up. Place in a buttered dish and cover with the rest of the white wine. Cover with parchment paper and cook gently for 90 minutes, basting often.

To serve, cut into slices, because the bones have been removed.

♀ Pouilly-Fuissé, white Mâcon, Pouilly-Fumé

LOTTE À LA BORDELAISE

MONKFISH BORDELAISE

Nicknamed anglerfish or sea devil, monkfish is always sold with the head cut off.

1 (1-INCH) SLICE
    MONKFISH PER
    PERSON
OLIVE OIL
2 OR 3 TOMATOES
1 SHALLOT
THYME
1 GLASS MADEIRA
1 GLASS DRY WHITE
    WINE
SALT
PEPPER
CROUTONS
GARLIC

Wipe and dry the slices of monkfish. Put in a frying pan with 4 or 5 spoons of oil, depending on how much fish you have. Warm the oil and fry the slices of monkfish on both sides.

Take them out. Put in more oil and the tomatoes, peeled, seeded, and cut in quarters. Add a finely chopped shallot, thyme, the Madeira, the dry white wine, salt, and pepper. Cook over a high flame until the tomatoes are reduced to a puree.

Place the slices of monkfish back in the pan and leave to cook gently for 15 minutes on very low heat.

Serve with croutons fried in oil and lightly rubbed with garlic.

♀ White Mâcon

LOTTE RÔTIE AU CURRY

ROASTED MONKFISH WITH CURRY

Monkfish can be cooked in the oven with a sauce, or as kebabs, as its flesh—fine and firm—behaves like meat.

1 (2.25-LB) MONKFISH
    TAIL
2 GLASSES DRY
    WHITE WINE
BUTTER
SALT
PEPPER
7 PINTS MUSSELS
RICE
2 TEASPOONS CURRY
    POWDER
CAYENNE PEPPER
BEURRE MANIÉ
    (PAGE 254)
2 EGG YOLKS

Take the skin off the monkfish tail, trim, wash, and drain. Put in a gratin dish with the dry white wine, 2 glasses of water, a good piece of butter, salt, and pepper. Leave to cook gently for 30 minutes, depending on size.

Steam open the mussels, and take out of their shells. Add their cooking liquor to that of the monkfish (being careful not to pour in the sand that can often be found at the bottom of the casserole).

Make a pilaf rice seasoned with salt, curry powder, and a pinch of cayenne pepper.

Reduce the cooking liquor from the monkfish, along with that of the mussels, by half. Bind it with the *beurre manié*, and add the egg yolks, whisking vigorously. At the last minute, add in a good piece of butter.

Arrange the monkfish, surrounded by the mussels and the rice. Serve the sauce to the side.

♀ Pouilly-Fuissé, white Mâcon

(Over) Mathieu Viannay, the current head chef at La Mère Brazier, Lyon

MERLANS À LA DIEPPOISE

WHITING DIEPPOISE

MUSSELS
MUSHROOMS
WHITE WINE
BOUQUET GARNI
1 (7-OZ) WHITING PER
  PERSON
BEURRE MANIÉ
  (PAGE 254)
HEAVY CREAM
SALT
PEPPER

Cook the mussels and mushrooms in a court bouillon made up of white wine, water, bouquet garni. Take out and keep warm.

Split each whiting down its back, lift out the bones, and gut. Poach gently in the simmering (not boiling) court bouillon. When the fish are cooked, take them out and keep warm on a plate.

Reduce the court bouillon and bind with the *beurre manié*. Add a few spoons of heavy cream. Adjust the seasoning.

Pour the sauce over the whiting and garnish with the mushrooms and mussels.

♓ Muscadet

MERLANS FRITS COLBERT

FRIED WHITING COLBERT

1 (7-OZ) WHITING PER
  PERSON
1 EGG
BREAD CRUMBS
OIL FOR FRYING
LEMON
PARSLEY
BEURRE MAÎTRE
  D'HÔTEL (PAGE
  253)
TARRAGON

Clean the fish carefully. Split down the back of each to take out the bone. Dip in a beaten egg and dredge in bread crumbs to cover well. Deep-fry.

Drain on absorbent paper. Surround with quarters of lemon and whole parsley, briefly deep-fried.

Serve with the *beurre maître d'hôtel* into which you have added a soupspoon of chopped tarragon. Serve with steamed potatoes.

♓ White Mâcon, Muscadet

BRANDADE DE MORUE

SALT COD TOASTS

There are other ways of making a brandade—with a pestle and mortar in particular. This method is easy. Morue *and* cabillaud *are the same fish.* Cabillaud *is fresh cod, while the* morue *is salted or dried cod.*

14 OZ SALT COD
1½ CUPS OLIVE OIL,
  PLUS EXTRA FOR
  FRYING
1 CLOVE GARLIC
1 CUP MILK
SALT
PEPPER
BREAD

De-salt the cod at least 24 hours ahead by putting it in a sieve inside a bigger casserole full of water—the salt cod must not touch the bottom so that the salt can wash off cleanly.

Poach, covered, for 12 minutes in fresh water. Take out, lift off the skin and bones, and flake off the flesh.

In a cast-iron pan warm ½ cup of the olive oil. When it is boiling, add the salt-cod flakes and work with a wooden spoon to shred them.

Add in a crushed clove of garlic. Slowly incorporate, working the spoon vigorously, the remaining olive oil and the boiling milk. It should have the same consistency as a thick puree of potatoes. Adjust the seasoning and don't spare the pepper.

Sauté some bread slices in olive oil and spread the mix on top. Put under a broiler for a few minutes.

♀ White Mâcon

MORUE FORESTIÈRE

SALT COD WITH TRUFFLES

This dish used to be made in areas where there were truffles. One hesitates, these days, to pair such an ordinary fish with truffles paid for in gold.

1 LB SALT COD
MUSHROOMS
FRESH TRUFFLES
BUTTER
SAUCE HOLLANDAISE
  (PAGE 257)
HEAVY CREAM

Choose a good, white, thick piece of salt cod. De-salt the night before, as for *Brandade de Morue* (page 125). Poach in fresh water for 12 minutes. Take out and lift off the skin and flake the flesh off the bones.

Sweat some sliced mushrooms with a fine julienne of truffles in butter. Turn into a well-buttered gratin dish. Cover this bed with the pieces of salt cod cut as scallops. Cover again with a layer of mushrooms and truffles. Warm in the oven for a few minutes and sauce with the hollandaise filled out with a little heavy cream.

Place under a red-hot broiler to color the sauce without letting it turn.

♇ White Mâcon

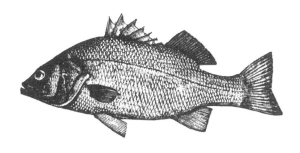

MORUE À LA NIÇOISE

SALT COD NICOISE

14 OZ SALT COD
PÂTE À FRIRE
  (PAGE 245)
OIL FOR FRYING
POTATOES
OLIVE OIL
2 OR 3 ONIONS
1 CLOVE GARLIC
1 LARGE TOMATO
BOUQUET GARNI
GREEN AND BLACK
  OLIVES

De-salt the cod at least 24 hours ahead, as for *Brandade de Morue* (page 125).

Carefully take out and lift off the skin and flake the flesh off the bones. Cut into large chunks. Dredge the fish through the *pâte à frire* (frying batter) and deep-fry. Take out and keep warm. Put some potatoes on to steam.

In a frying pan, fry in olive oil the finely chopped onions, a clove of garlic, and the tomato—peeled, seeded, and cut into quarters. Moisten with 2 cups of water. Add the potatoes, cut into quarters, the bouquet garni, and pitted green and black olives. Leave to cook slowly, very slowly.

Ten minutes before serving, add the pieces of salt cod to the frying pan, being careful not to break them.

Serve in a large dish, potatoes underneath, cod on top. Serve very hot.

♈ Rosé du Var

HARENGS FRAIS MARINÉS

MARINATED FRESH HERRING

HERRINGS
SALT
DRY WHITE WINE
LEMON
CELERY
CARROTS
ONIONS
PEPPER

Gut and scale the herrings. Sprinkle with salt and leave for an hour.

Meanwhile, make a court bouillon, bringing the white wine to a boil seasoned with lemon, chopped celery, carrots, onions, salt, and pepper. Put the herrings in this mix without letting them cook completely.

Take the herrings out and arrange in a stoneware dish. Cover with the warm court bouillon and, on the surface, float a couple of lemon rounds. Hermetically seal the dish.

♟ Dry white

HARENGS FRAIS EN RAGOÛT

RAGOUT OF HERRING

Herring is at its best before spawning, between October and January.

HERRINGS
BUTTER
COARSE RED WINE
SALT
PEPPER
SMALL ONIONS
GARLIC
1 BAY LEAF
ROUX (PAGE 263)
CROUTONS

Gut and scale the herrings. Warm in a pan with some butter for a moment and then cover with an equal amount of rough red wine and water; salt, pepper. Add in the small onions, garlic, and bay. Leave to cook gently, without boiling, for 20 to 30 minutes.

Make a roux. Moisten with a little of the cooking liquor from the fish. Allow it to thicken and pour over the fish a few minutes before serving.

Serve very hot with croutons fried in butter and lightly rubbed with garlic.

♟ Red

HARENGS GRILLÉS SAUCE MOUTARDE

BROILED HERRINGS WITH MUSTARD SAUCE

1 HERRING
  PER PERSON
SALT
PEPPER
OLIVE OIL
ROUX (PAGE 263)
1 GLASS MILK
2 SOUPSPOONS
  MUSTARD
2 SOUPSPOONS
  HEAVY CREAM
2 EGG YOLKS

Scale the herrings. Split them down their backs to lift out the bones, which will also allow for a shorter cooking time. Gut them. Season them with salt and pepper, and wipe over with olive oil. Broil.

In a thick casserole, make a roux with ¼ cup of butter and ½ cup of flour. Thicken with a good glass of boiling milk and leave to cook for 10 minutes, stirring.

Take off the heat and incorporate, whisking energetically, the mustard, heavy cream, and egg yolks. If this sauce is to be reheated, it absolutely must not boil.

Serve the sauce over the herrings straight from the broiler.

♇ Rosé de Provence

GENDARMES EN SURPRISE

STUFFED HERRING

HERRING
POTATO PUREE
BUTTER
HEAVY CREAM

Open the herrings and carefully take out all the bones. Stuff the herrings with a puree of potatoes, well buttered, and to which you have added a spoon of heavy cream.

Wrap each fish in a sheet of aluminum foil. Cook under the broiler.

Serve the herrings in their shirts.

♇ Muscadet, Sancerre

FILETS DE MAQUEREAUX
À LA MODE DE FÉCAMP

MACKEREL FILLETS FÉCAMP

*Mackerel are usually fished between March and November
when, on important banks, they come near shore.*

2 FINE MACKEREL,
   FILLETED
BUTTER
3 GLASSES DRY WHITE
   WINE
2 SHALLOTS
SALT
PEPPER
7 LB MUSSELS
BEURRE MANIÉ
   (PAGE 254)
HEAVY CREAM
LEMON
PARSLEY

Wash the fillets of mackerel. Place them in a gratin dish, well
buttered, with 2 glasses of dry white wine, finely chopped
shallots, salt, and pepper. Place in the oven for 10 minutes.

Steam open the mussels separately, with a glass of white
wine. Take the mussels out of their shells and add them to the
mackerel, along with their cooking liquor.

Lift out the mackerel and mussels and keep them warm. Reduce
the cooking liquor by half. Bind with the *beurre manié*. Add a
few spoons of heavy cream, salt, pepper, and a squeeze of lemon.

Arrange the mussels around the mackerel and pour over the
sauce. Garnish with chopped parsley. Serve very hot.

♈ White Mâcon, Muscadet

(Opposite) La Mère—always happiest in her kitchen

ANGUILLES À LA CHARENTAISE

EEL CHARENTE

Eels are, above all, an estuary fish. They only head for the sea to reproduce between March and April.

EELS
1 CLOVE GARLIC
2 SHALLOTS
2 ONIONS
BUTTER
2 SPOONS FLOUR
WHITE WINE
SALT
PEPPER
1 PINCH SUGAR

Carefully skin and clean the eels and chop into large pieces.

Rough-chop the garlic, shallots, onions, and warm through in butter in a frying pan. Add the flour and let everything brown lightly, stirring with a wooden spoon. Cover with one-quarter white wine to three-quarters water. Salt, pepper, and leave to cook for 30 minutes.

Now add the pieces of eel and the sugar, and leave to cook for another 20 minutes. Serve very hot.

♈ Muscadet

ANGUILLES AU VERT À LA FLAMANDE

FLEMISH GREEN EELS

4.5 LB SMALL,
   SKINNED EELS
BUTTER
BEER
3.5 OZ WASHED
   SORREL
2 TABLESPOONS
   BLANCHED NETTLES
3.5 OZ PARSLEY
1 TEASPOON SAGE
1 TEASPOON SAVORY
1 TEASPOON
   TARRAGON
SALT
PEPPER
CORNSTARCH

Cut the eels into 2 to 3-inch-long pieces. Warm through in butter in a frying pan. Cover with beer. Add in the sorrel, the nettles, chopped parsley, the sage, savory, tarragon; salt and pepper. Allow to boil for 15 minutes.

Take out the pieces of eel and keep them warm. Dilute a little cornstarch with the warm beer and add in to bind the sauce.

Serve hot with its sauce or cold with heavy cream.

♈ Beer

BROCHET À LA BORDELAISE

PIKE BORDELAISE

1 PIKE, ABOUT 7 OZ
  PER PERSON
ONIONS
CARROTS
THYME
BAY LEAF
PARSLEY
1 BOTTLE RED
  BORDEAUX
BEURRE MANIÉ
  (PAGE 254)
SALT
PEPPER
CROUTONS
GARLIC

Clean the pike and cut into portions—1 per person.

Make a mirepoix with roughly chopped onions and carrots. Warm through in butter with thyme, bay, and parsley stalks in a frying pan.

Put the pieces of pike on the mirepoix and cover with a good Bordeaux. As the liquid starts to shimmer, lift out the pieces of pike and keep warm in a gratin dish. Reduce the cooking liquid and bind with the *beurre manié*. Check the seasoning.

Sieve the sauce over the fish. Serve with a few croutons, lightly rubbed with garlic. Sprinkle with chopped parsley. Serve with steamed potatoes.

♈ Any dry white wine

SUPRÊME DE BROCHET À LA DIJONNAISE

DIJON PIKE FILLETS

1 FINE SAÔNE PIKE,
  ABOUT 6.5 LB
FATTY BACON
BOUQUET GARNI
SHALLOTS
PARSLEY
THYME
BAY LEAF
SALT
PEPPER
1 GLASS COGNAC
1 GLASS MADEIRA
1 GLASS DRY WHITE
  WINE
MUSHROOMS
HEAVY CREAM
BUTTER

Take the fillets off the pike. Lift off both skins and carefully pick over for any bones. Slip some fatty bacon into the fillets the same way a butcher might for a roast of beef. Leave to marinate with the bouquet garni, 2 chopped shallots, the parsley stalks, thyme, bay, salt, pepper, Cognac, Madeira, white wine—enough to cover. After 1 or 2 days, take the fillets out, drain, and wipe dry.

Butter well a long gratin dish. Put the fillets in the dish with finely chopped mushrooms. Pour over enough marinade to come halfway up the fillets. Bake in a reasonably hot oven for about 20 minutes, basting often.

When the fillets are well colored, add a few spoons of heavy cream and a few pieces of butter.

♈ Meursault, Chablis

BROCHET AU BEURRE BLANC

PIKE BEURRE BLANC

1 (6.5-LB) PIKE
CARROTS
ONIONS
SALT
PEPPERCORNS
THYME
BAY LEAF
GARLIC
WHITE WINE (FROM
   THE LOIRE IN
   PRINCIPAL)
WINE VINEGAR
PARSLEY
4 SHALLOTS
2 CUPS BUTTER

Clean the pike. Wash it and wrap in clean linen. Place in a fish kettle.

In a large casserole, put chopped carrots and onions. Add salt, peppercorns, thyme, bay, and garlic. Leave to cook for 10 minutes.

Add the white wine and the vinegar. Leave to cook for another 15 minutes and allow to cool a little.

Pour this court bouillon over the pike and cook over a lively heat. As soon as it starts to boil, lower the fire: The fish must cook, without boiling, for 25 minutes.

Make the *beurre blanc*: In a thick-bottomed saucepan, reduce by half a good glass of wine vinegar, finely chopped shallots, salt, and a grind of pepper. Whisk and add, piece by piece, the cold butter. To succeed, the mix must be very white and smooth.

Drain the pike and take the skin off both sides. Serve on hot plates, covered with its *beurre blanc*.

♇ Sancerre, Muscadet

CARPE DE LA DOMBES FARCIE

STUFFED CARP

1 (6.5-LB) CARP
3.5 OZ MUSHROOMS
BUTTER
SHALLOTS
1 LB QUENELLES DE
  BROCHET (PAGE 51)
TRUFFLES
PARSLEY
SALT
PEPPER
2 BOTTLES DRY
  WHITE WINE
BREAD CRUMBS

Carefully take off any of the big scales from the carp. Split down the back of the fish and take out the backbone and all the little bones that are attached. Gut. Keep the roe, if you find any.

Chop the mushrooms finely and warm through in butter. Chop the shallots and warm through in butter for a few seconds.

Make a stuffing with the *quenelles de brochet*, the mushrooms, the shallots, chopped truffle, chopped parsley, and the roe of the carp. Salt, pepper, mix well, and fill the carp. Sew up tightly with a strong string/cotton.

Place in a gratin dish. Cover with white wine, a few nuts of butter and bread crumbs. Cook in a medium oven for 2 hours.

To serve, take off the string. Carve the fish into slices and baste with the cooking juices.

♈ Meursault, Chablis

MEURETTE DE BOURGOGNE

BURGUNDY RED WINE FISH STEW

1 SMALL EEL
1 YOUNG PIKE
1 SMALL CARP
2 TROUT
1 BOTTLE YOUNG
  BURGUNDY RED
  WINE
1 LARGE ONION
BOUQUET GARNI
PARSLEY
A FEW CLOVES
5 CLOVES GARLIC
2 GLASSES COGNAC
BEURRE MANIÉ
  (PAGE 254)
BREAD

Buy live fish to be sure they are fresh.

Clean the fish, gut, and cut into portions.

Bring 1 quart of red wine to the boil in a large earthenware casserole with the chopped onion, the bouquet garni, the parsley, a few cloves, and 4 cloves of crushed garlic. Put the pieces of fish in. The fish should be covered by the wine. Bring to a boil over a high flame. Add the Cognac. Leave to cook for 15 minutes over a good flame and then turn it down to a gentle heat.

Bind the sauce with the *beurre manié*, and leave to bubble for 10 minutes.

Toast some bread, rub with garlic, and place in a bowl. Lay the pieces of fish on the bread.

Take out the bouquet garni and other seasonings from the sauce. Add in a few pieces of butter and pour over the fish.

℣ Beaujolais nouveau

POCHOUSE DES BORDS DE SAÔNE

SAÔNE POACHER'S STEW

Any mix of freshwater fish can go into this stew—whatever someone has caught after a day's fishing.

1 (2-LB) PIKE
1 GOOD EEL
1 FAT PERCH
1 FAT TENCH
4.5 OZ BACON
13 CLOVES GARLIC
THYME
TARRAGON
SALT
PEPPER
DRY WHITE WINE
BEURRE MANIÉ
   (PAGE 254)
BAGUETTE
BUTTER

Scale, gut, and wash the recently caught fish. Cut up into portions.

Put in the bottom of a cast-iron casserole the bacon, cut into dice, 12 crushed garlic cloves, the thyme, and the tarragon. Lay the fish on this bed, salt, pepper, and cover with a light, dry Mâcon. Cook over a hot flame.

When it starts to boil, bind the sauce with the *beurre manié* and let it bubble for 30 minutes, stirring occasionally.

Cut croutons from the baguette, rub with garlic, and fry in butter. Put the croutons in a big tureen, put the fish on top, and sieve the sauce over them. Serve very hot.

Ⴤ Pouilly-Fuissé

TRUITE AU BLEU

BLUE TROUT

This traditional recipe is very cruel, as you must use live trout. It was not designed for sensitive souls. The effect of the vinegar is to make the skin turn blue. Some people do not like the skin of the trout, in which case lift it off before serving.

CARROTS
ONIONS
SALT
PEPPERCORNS
PARSLEY
1 BOTTLE DRY
   WHITE WINE
1 GLASS VINEGAR
1 (7-OZ) TROUT
   PER PERSON
BUTTER
LEMON

Poach in water for 10 minutes, chopped carrots and onions, salt, peppercorns, and parsley stalks. Add the white wine and a good glass of vinegar. Pour this court bouillon into a fish kettle.

Ten minutes before serving, take the trout—still alive—out of the tank, gut them quickly, wash, and plunge into the boiling court bouillon. They will twist and the flesh will break on all sides—5 minutes cooking is enough.

Take the fish out and serve on plates with napkins. Serve with melted salted butter, a squeeze of lemon, and parsley—or a nut of *Sauce Hollandaise* (page 257)—and some steamed potatoes.

♈ Gewürztraminer, Riesling

TRUITE GRILLÉE À LA RIBEAUVILLÉ

BROILED TROUT RIBEAUVILLÉ

It is preferable to serve the sauce separately rather than over the fish, depending on taste . . . it is easier anyway. Ribeauvillé is a town in Alsace.

SAUCE BÉARNAISE
   (PAGE 255)
TOMATO PUREE
ANCHOVY PUREE
1 (7-OZ) TROUT
   PER PERSON
SALT
OIL

Make the *béarnaise* and add in the tomato and anchovy purees.

Scale the trout, wash, and pat dry. With a very sharp knife, make a few cuts in the side of the fish. Salt inside and out. Wipe with oil. Broil on a high heat.

Serve accompanied by its *sauce béarnaise.*

♈ Gewurztraminer, Riesling

TRUITE À LA MOLLAU

TROUT MOLLAU

1 (9-OZ) TROUT PER
  PERSON
SMALL ONIONS
BUTTER
ALSACE WINE
SALT
PEPPER
BAY LEAF
CLOVES
GARLIC
PARSLEY
BUTTER
BREAD

It is best to use a river trout for this recipe.

Carefully clean the trout. Rinse in clean water, wipe dry.

Warm the chopped onions in butter. Add in half wine and half water, enough so the fish will be covered. Add salt, pepper, bay, cloves, garlic, and parsley. Let this court bouillon cook for 10 minutes.

Place the trout in the bouillon and let cook another 10 minutes.

Take out the trout and place on a plate. Sauce with browned butter, in which you have fried a little finely chopped bread. Add a glass of the court bouillon.

Serve very hot.

♈ Riesling, Gewürztraminer

TRUITE À L'AMIRAL

ADMIRAL'S TROUT

MUSHROOMS
SALT
PEPPER
LEMON
1 (9-OZ) TROUT,
  CLEANED,
  PER PERSON
1 GLASS DRY
  WHITE WINE
BEURRE MANIÉ
  (PAGE 254)
2 SOUPSPOONS
  BEURRE
  D'ÉCREVISSES
  (PAGE 253)
2 SPOONS HEAVY
  CREAM
BUTTER
TRUFFLE

Quarter the mushrooms and cook in a little salted water with a grind of pepper and a squeeze of lemon.

Take out the mushrooms and put the trout in to cook in the same liquid. Add the dry white wine and cook slowly, very slowly.

After cooking, take the trout out and peel the skin from both sides. Keep warm in a gratin dish. Reduce the cooking liquid and bind it with the *beurre manié*. Incorporate the *beurre d'écrevisses*, the heavy cream, and a nut of fresh butter.

Decorate the trout with the mushrooms and slices of truffle. Check the seasoning of the sauce and pour over the fish.

♈ Alsace, white Arbois

LES VOLAILLES
ET LE GIBIER
POULTRY
AND GAME

VOLAILLE DEMI-DEUIL

CHICKEN IN HALF-MOURNING

This perhaps most famous recipe from Mère Brazier originated with Mère Filloux. The secret lies in the quality of the chicken. Her chef Roger Garnier cooked chickens like this every day for twenty years. It is cooked in a faitout—*literally a do-it-all pan. The cooking time is quite short for such a large chicken and la Mère wisely recommends leaving the chicken to stand a further 30 minutes, and possibly a bit longer.*

1 FINE TRUFFLE
1 FINE BRESSE
    CHICKEN (OR ANY
    HIGH-QUALITY
    CHICKEN) OF LESS
    THAN A YEAR,
    WEIGHING ABOUT
    3.25 LB
CARROTS
LEEKS
MUSTARD
GHERKINS
GIROTTE PLUMS
    IN VINEGAR
SEA SALT

Slice the truffle across into circles about ⅛ inch thick. Slip the slices under the skin of the breast and thighs of the chicken. Fold up the chicken in a tight muslin cloth. Tie it up with string under the wings and thighs to keep it in place.

In a large casserole—a *faitout*—put some carrots and the leeks. Fill it halfway with water. Bring to a boil. As the water bubbles plunge the chicken in and make sure it is just covered by the water. Leave to cook gently for 45 minutes.

It is a good idea to leave the chicken in its broth for 30 minutes before serving. Serve the chicken simply with its vegetables out on the table with mustard, gherkins, Girotte plums in vinegar, and sea salt.

♉ Beaujolais nouveau

VELOUTÉ DE VOLAILLE FAÇON MÈRE BRAZIER

MÈRE BRAZIER'S CHICKEN SOUP

La Mère would often cook this for her old regulars—a velouté based on a chicken consommé. She would make it from the leftover stock from her Volaille Demi-Deuil *(left). The stock is the basis of this* velouté, *which is one reason it became famous.*

CHICKEN
   CONSOMMÉ
TAPIOCA
HEAVY CREAM
SALT
PEPPER
2 EGG YOLKS
TRUFFLES
   (IF YOU HAVE THEM)

Cook a few spoons of the tapioca in a not-too-salty chicken consommé.

Add into this broth a quarter again of good heavy cream. Adjust the seasoning and, just before serving, whisk in the egg yolks—away from the heat. You can add a julienne of fresh truffles. Serve in very hot bowls.

POULET AU CHAMPAGNE

CHICKEN BRAISED IN CHAMPAGNE

1 (3.25-LB) CHICKEN
BUTTER
4 CLOVES GARLIC
SALT
PEPPER
4 GLASSES BRUT
   CHAMPAGNE

Take off the chicken wings, breasts, and thighs, and cut the carcass into pieces. In a frying pan, warm a good piece of butter and fry the quarters of chicken and the pieces of carcass.

Add the unpeeled cloves of garlic; salt, pepper.

When everything is well colored, deglaze with a glass of Champagne. Repeat the process a few minutes later and leave to cook slowly for 35 to 40 minutes.

Baste the chicken quarters with 2 glasses of Champagne.

Take out the carcass pieces and the garlic from the pan, and reduce the liquid. At the last moment, add a good piece of butter and whisk energetically. Pour the sauce over the pieces of chicken.

Serve with artichoke bottoms fried in butter and filled with sautéed mushrooms.

♏ Brut Champagne

POULET AU SANG
À LA BERRICHONNE

BERRY CHICKEN

Save the blood from the chicken by adding half a glass of wine vinegar. You probably will not be able to get fresh blood today, but you might add blood sausage instead.

1 (3.5-LB) CHICKEN
  WITH ITS BLOOD
BUTTER
6 SMALL ONIONS
SALT
PEPPER
2 SPOONS FLOUR
1 GLASS WHITE WINE
BOUQUET GARNI
2 CLOVES GARLIC

In a frying pan, fry the 4 quarters of the chicken in butter. Add the chopped onions and let both color. Salt, pepper, and sift over the flour. Let it brown, wet with white wine and a glass of water. Add the bouquet garni and unpeeled cloves of garlic. Leave to cook slowly, covered, for around 35 minutes.

Arrange the chicken pieces on a plate.

Add the blood to the pan over a soft flame, without letting it boil, and sieve the sauce over the chicken.

Serve with fresh noodles or fondant potatoes.

♉ Red Coteaux de la Loire

POULET À LA CRÈME AUX MORILLES

CHICKEN WITH MORELS AND CREAM

1 FINE BRESSE
  CHICKEN (OR ANY
  HIGH-QUALITY
  CHICKEN)
SALT
PEPPER
FLOUR
MORELS
BUTTER
2 CUPS HEAVY CREAM
LEMON (OPTIONAL)

Chop the bird into four. Take out the bones from the wings and thighs. Take off the parson's nose. Salt, pepper, and flour. In a frying pan, cook all 4 pieces in butter.

While the chicken is cooking, let the morels breathe in some melted butter.

When the chicken is cooked, lift out the pieces and deglaze the pan with the cream. Put the chicken pieces back, leave to bubble a few minutes, and bring back to a boil. Check the seasoning of the sauce. You can, depending on taste, add a few drops of lemon juice.

Lay up the chicken pieces on a plate. Cover with the morels. Sieve the sauce over and serve straightaway, without putting it in the oven.

Serve with a plate of rice, which goes very well with the cream sauce.

♀ Beaujolais nouveau, Côtes-du-Rhône

POULET BONNE FEMME

CHICKEN BONNE FEMME

1 (3.25-LB) CHICKEN
SALT
PEPPER
3.5 OZ SAUSAGE
  MEAT
CHICKEN LIVER
WHITE CRUSTLESS
  BREAD
MILK
PARSLEY
BACON FAT
BUTTER
12 SMALL ONIONS
STREAKY BACON
POTATOES

Salt and pepper the inside of the bird. Stuff with the sausage meat, mixed with chopped chicken livers and the bread soaked in milk and pressed out. Add chopped parsley. Sew up the bird and truss. Cover with bacon fat and slow-fry in butter in a cocotte.

Add the onions and some streaky lardons. Keep turning the chicken to color it all over. Leave to cook for 30 minutes, then add in cubes of potato.

Finish the cooking in a medium oven, adding a glass of water and leaving uncovered.

Before serving, take off the bacon and the string. Cut up the chicken.

Arrange the chicken pieces back in the cocotte, on top of the potatoes, and decorate each piece with a spoon of stuffing.

♀ All red wines

146

COQ AU CHAMBERTIN

CHICKEN IN CHAMBERTIN

1 (3.5-LB) CHICKEN
SALT
PEPPER
FLOUR
BACON
BUTTER
1 SHALLOT
1 CARROT
1 SPRIG THYME
RED WINE
  (PREFERABLY
  CHAMBERTIN OR
  PINOT NOIR)
BEURRE MANIÉ
  (PAGE 254)
MUSHROOMS
BUTTER

Cut the chicken in four. Take out the leg bones and the wing bones. Season the pieces with salt and pepper, and dredge in flour.

In a small cocotte—a *coquille*—brown some bacon lardons in butter. Take them out when they are colored and keep them ready.

Put a diced shallot in the cocotte, a diced carrot, a sprig of thyme, and the chicken pieces. Brown the chicken pieces, then cover with Burgundy or a good, acidic red wine. The wine should be warmed first. Leave to bubble for about an hour.

Take out the chicken pieces and keep warm. Bind the sauce with the *beurre manié*. Check the seasoning, which should be quite peppery.

At the last moment, add a good piece of butter and whisk energetically. Sieve the sauce over the chicken. Slice and sauté some mushrooms in butter, and add to the chicken with the lardons.

Serve with fresh noodles or steamed potatoes.

♈ Red Burgundy, Châteauneuf-du-Pape, red Bordeaux

POULET AUX ÉCREVISSES

CHICKEN WITH CRAYFISH

20 CRAYFISH
OLIVE OIL
CARROTS
SHALLOTS
COGNAC
WHITE WINE
PEPPER
CAYENNE PEPPER
TOMATO PUREE
BEURRE MANIÉ
   (PAGE 254)
1 (3.25-LB) CHICKEN
SALT
FLOUR
BUTTER
2 CUPS HEAVY CREAM
CORNSTARCH
   (OPTIONAL)

Sweat the crayfish in oil, in a frying pan, with chopped carrots and shallots. Deglaze with warm Cognac and flambé. Cover with white wine and season with pepper, cayenne, and tomato puree. Cook, covered, for 10 minutes. Take out the crayfish, and shell all but 4. Reduce the cooking liquid and bind with the *beurre manié*.

Cut the chicken into four. Salt, pepper, and flour, and sauté in hot butter without totally coloring them. When the pieces are well started, cover and leave to cook for 35 to 40 minutes. Arrange the 4 quarters of chicken on a hot plate.

Deglaze the frying pan with the cream and a little of the sauce from the crayfish. Add some pepper and bind with cornstarch if needed.

Plate the crayfish, and pour over the sauce through a sieve. Decorate with the 4 crayfish still in their shells.

Serve with a good, curried rice on—as always—very hot plates.

♀ Beaujolais, Côte-Rôtie, Hermitage

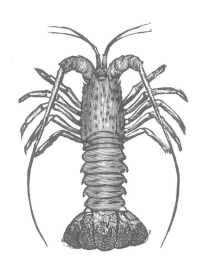

POULET SAUTÉ CHASSEUR

HUNTER'S CHICKEN

1 (3.25-LB) CHICKEN
SALT
PEPPER
OIL
BUTTER
5 OZ MUSHROOMS
1 SHALLOT
2 GLASSES WHITE
   WINE
2 SPOONS TOMATO
   PUREE
CORNSTARCH
   (OPTIONAL)
CHERVIL
TARRAGON
PARSLEY

Take the 4 quarters off the chicken, salt and pepper them, and fry in oil and butter. When they are well colored, cover and leave to cook for 30 minutes.

Add in chopped mushrooms and finely chopped shallot. Leave to cook another 10 minutes.

Take out the chicken pieces and keep warm.

Leave the mushrooms in the frying pan. Deglaze with white wine and tomato puree. Check the seasoning of the sauce. Bind lightly with cornstarch if necessary. Add a tablespoon of chopped chervil and tarragon. Pour the sauce on the chicken and garnish with chopped parsley.

This can be accompanied with rice and artichoke bottoms filled with mushrooms.

♀ Tavel, rosé de Provence, Beaujolais nouveau

POULET DE GRAIN FRIT

FRIED FREE-RANGE CHICKEN

A chicken that has not been gutted should not be kept more than 24 hours, even in the refrigerator.

1 (1.75-LB) FREE-
  RANGE CHICKEN
1 GLASS WHITE WINE
OIL
THYME
BAY LEAF
LEMON JUICE
PARSLEY
SALT
PEPPER
1 EGG
FLOUR
BREAD CRUMBS
BUTTER
LEMON
SAUCE BÉARNAISE
  (PAGE 255)

Take off the 4 parts of the chicken and take out the bones from the legs and wings. Marinate for an hour or two in white wine, olive oil, thyme, bay, lemon juice, parsley, salt, and pepper.

Drain, wipe dry, dip in egg, and dredge in the flour and bread crumbs. Cook in a frying pan, in hot butter, turning a few times. Allow about 25 minutes to cook.

Drain well and put the chicken on a plate with rounds of lemon and chopped parsley.

Serve a well-seasoned *sauce béarnaise* to the side.

Accompany with seasonal vegetables, Provençal tomatoes, or fries.

♀ All red wines

POULET FARCI À LA CERVELLE

CHICKEN STUFFED WITH BRAINS

CALF'S BRAIN
SALT
PEPPER
1 (3.5-LB) CHICKEN
BUTTER

Clean the calf's brain in cold water for a few hours. Take it out; salt and pepper. Then salt and pepper the inside of the chicken and put the brain inside. Sew and truss the chicken. Butter the outsides well and roast in the oven.

Carve the chicken in four and set on a plate around the brain in the middle. Serve the jus to the side. Each piece of chicken should be served with a slice of brain.

Serve with seasonal vegetables.

♀ All red wines

POULET GRILLÉ BÉARNAISE

GRILLED CHICKEN WITH SAUCE BÉARNAISE

We recommend a chicken from Allier—in the Vichy—because its skin is better than those from Bresse.

1 ALLIER CHICKEN
SALT
PEPPER
1 EGG
BREAD CRUMBS
OIL
BUTTER
SAUCE BÉARNAISE
(PAGE 255)

Split the chicken in four. Lift off the forked bone in the wings and the front thighbone. Salt, pepper, and dip in beaten egg. Then dredge in the bread crumbs.

Put a little oil in a cast-iron pan. Put in the 4 chicken pieces and, on each, a piece of butter. Put in a hot oven for about 45 minutes.

While it is cooking, make the *sauce béarnaise*, which should be well seasoned and ready in time for the chicken.

When the chicken is cooked, lay the pieces on a plate with Provençal tomatoes and some small rissole potatoes.

♆ Châteauneuf-du-Pape, red Hermitage, light Burgundy

POULET SAUTÉ AUX CÈPES

BRAISED CHICKEN WITH PORCINI MUSHROOMS

If you do not have fresh porcini at your disposal, you can experiment with other full-flavored wild mushrooms.

12 FIRM-HEADED
 PORCINI
 MUSHROOMS
OLIVE OIL
1 (3.5-LB) CHICKEN
SALT
PEPPER
BUTTER
2 GLASSES WHITE
 WINE
BACON
PARSLEY
1 CLOVE GARLIC

Wash the mushrooms in clean water a few times, drain, and cook in olive oil for 10 minutes.

Take off the 4 quarters of the chicken, salt and pepper them, and fry in butter. As soon as they are colored, add the mushrooms. Wet with white wine and add a little bacon, chopped, with parsley and garlic. Cover and leave to cook for 30 minutes.

Set up the chicken pieces on a plate, surround with mushrooms and Provençal tomatoes. Pour over the sauce. Serve on hot plates.

♆ Light red Bordeaux, Côte-Rôtie, Hermitage

POULET SAUTÉ AUX DUCS DE BOURGOGNE

CHICKEN SAUTÉ FOR THE DUKES OF BURGUNDY

1 (3.5-LB) CHICKEN
SALT
PEPPER
BUTTER
1 GLASS PORT
1 GLASS COGNAC
1 GLASS WHISKEY
1 GLASS KIRSCH
2 EGG YOLKS
2 CUPS HEAVY CREAM

Take the 4 quarters off the chicken and salt and pepper them. Start by frying them in butter to color, and then cook them slowly in the oven for 40 minutes.

Take the chicken pieces out and keep warm. Deglaze the roasting pan with the port, Cognac, whiskey, and kirsch. Let it reduce. Whisk the egg yolks into the heavy cream, and add into the jus. Let it cook for a few minutes, whisking energetically. Check the seasoning and sieve over the chicken.

Serve on very hot plates.

♉ Light red Burgundy, Hermitage, Côte-Rôtie

POULET SAUTÉ AU PORTO

CHICKEN WITH PORT

1 (3.5-LB) CHICKEN
SALT
BUTTER
1 GLASS COGNAC
1 GLASS PORT
MUSHROOMS
4 TABLESPOONS
   THICK HEAVY
   CREAM
PEPPER

Cut the chicken into four. Season with salt and put the pieces in a frying pan with butter, without letting them color too much. Wet with a small glass of Cognac and a good glass of port. Cover and leave to braise slowly for 35 to 40 minutes.

Quarter some mushrooms and sauté in butter.

Take out the chicken pieces and keep them warm. In the pan, put the heavy cream, salt, pepper, and add the mushrooms. Leave to simmer a few minutes, and return the chicken to the pan.

Serve from the pan, with rice.

♉ White Jura, light red

VOLAILLE DE BRESSE EN VESSIE AU RIESLING

BRESSE CHICKEN COOKED IN A PIG'S BLADDER WITH RIESLING

A good butcher may be able to find you a pig's bladder. You could also try to cook the chicken sous-vide.

1 PIG'S BLADDER
1 (3.5-LB) BRESSE
  CHICKEN
SEA SALT
4 CUPS RIESLING OR
  DRY WHITE WINE
LEEKS
CARROTS
TURNIPS

Wash the pig's bladder in a number of changes of cold water and soak overnight. Slip the chicken inside the bladder.

Salt lightly and fill the bladder with the Riesling or other dry white wine. Close up tightly with string. Cook in a marmite with 1 leek, 2 carrots, a good handful of sea salt, and enough water to cover the chicken.

Cook separately some carrots, turnips, and the whites of leeks to serve as garnish.

Open the bladder at the table so the guests can enjoy the smells of the Riesling and the chicken.

♀ Light Burgundy, Côte-Rôtie, red Hermitage

POULET SAUTÉ À LA PROVENÇALE

CHICKEN PROVENÇAL

1 (3.25-LB) CHICKEN
SALT
PEPPER
BUTTER
OLIVE OIL
1 SHALLOT
1 GLASS COGNAC
2 TOMATOES
1 SPRIG THYME
½ BAY LEAF
MUSHROOMS
PARSLEY

Take off the breast and legs, as usual, from the chicken, then season with salt and pepper. Warm in a frying pan, with a mix of butter and olive oil to color the pieces.

Add finely chopped shallot and flambé with warmed Cognac. Then add peeled and quartered tomatoes, the thyme, bay leaf, and diced raw mushrooms. Cover and leave to cook gently for 35 minutes.

Take out the thyme and bay leaf, add some chopped parsley, check the seasoning, and serve from the hot pan.

♀ Red or rosé from Provence

VOLAILLE JACQUARD

CHICKEN JACQUARD

1 PIG'S BLADDER
1 TRUFFLE
1 GLASS COGNAC
2 (4-LB) BRESSE
   CHICKENS
1 LEEK
1 STALK CELERY
1 SPRIG TARRAGON
SALT
PEPPER
3 TO 4 SPOONS
   THICK HEAVY
   CREAM
WHITE PEPPER

The night before, soak the pig's bladder in a number of changes of water.

Put the truffle in the glass of Cognac. Debone the chickens completely. Make a bouillon/consommé with the chicken bones, leek whites, celery, tarragon, salt, and pepper.

Put the meat from 1 bird into a grinder to make a stuffing. Working on a cold surface, or ice, add the heavy cream. Chop the truffle into tiny dice and add in. Season with salt and white pepper.

Use this stuffing to fill the second bird, re-forming it and sewing it up carefully. Slide the chicken into the pig's bladder and close up tightly with string.

Put your chicken bouillon into a cocotte and carefully place your stuffed chicken into it. Cook over a low flame, pricking the bladder with a needle every so often, to keep it from exploding. Allow at least 1 hour's cooking.

Serve the chicken in its bladder at the table.

Can be accompanied by rice or carrots and turnips poached in the bouillon.

♆ Burgundy, red Bordeaux, Côte-Rôtie

La Mère's Classic Menu No.4

Turbot au Chambertin
Turbot Cooked in Chambertin (page 116)

◆

Quenelles au Gratin
Quenelle Gratin

◆

Poulet Grillé Béarnaise
Grilled Chicken with Sauce Béarnaise
(page 151)

◆

Fromages de Saison
Seasonal Cheeses

◆

Tous les Desserts
Dessert of Your Choice

CANARD RÔTI FARCI

ROASTED DUCK STUFFED WITH OLIVES

Barbary ducks have more flesh than ordinary ducks. You
can put the duck liver into the potato and olive stuffing.

1 BARBARY DUCK
SALT
PEPPER
POTATOES
GREEN OLIVES
BUTTER

Salt and pepper the inside of the duck. Fill it with a hash of diced
potatoes and chopped olives. Sew up the opening. Put in a hot
oven in a cocotte with a little butter. Baste often and turn.

A few minutes before the end of the cooking, pour off the fat
and add some pitted olives. Then take the duck out, carve, and
arrange on a hot plate with the stuffing taken out of the carcass.

To make the jus, deglaze the cocotte with a glass of water, check
the seasoning, and pour over the duck. Serve a little stuffing with
each piece of duck.

♉ Châteauneuf-du-Pape, red Bordeaux

CANETON NANTAIS AUX NAVETS

NANTES DUCKLING WITH TURNIPS

1 (3-LB) DUCKLING
BUTTER
2 GLASSES DRY WHITE
    WINE
SALT
PEPPER
1 LB SMALL TURNIPS
5 OZ SMALL ONIONS
BOUQUET GARNI

Tie up the duckling and put in a cocotte with a little butter.
Brown it well all over and take out. Deglaze the cocotte with
2 glasses of white wine. Reduce and put the duck back in the
cocotte and cook over a gentle flame. Salt, pepper, and cover.

In another pan brown the turnips and onions in butter. When the
duck is about half cooked, add the turnips, the onions, and the
bouquet garni.

Carve the duck, arrange on a hot plate with its vegetables
around, and pour over the jus.

Serve on very hot plates.

♉ All red wines

DODINE DE CANARD, VOLAILLE, DINDE, OU FAISAN

DODINE OF DUCK, CHICKEN, TURKEY, OR PHEASANT

A ballotine is cooked in the same way as this, but covered with a mousseline and poached in a court bouillon. This recipe is a bit of a challenge. La Mère may well have bought such a dish from her charcutier. It is usually served cold.

1 DUCK, CHICKEN, TURKEY, OR PHEASANT
SALT
PEPPER
COGNAC
PORT
NECK OF PORK
VEAL FILLET
CHICKEN LIVERS
GOOSE OR DUCK LIVER
TRUFFLES
2 OR 3 EGGS
BUTTER

Choose a good bird, on the fatty side. Debone, starting along the back and taking care not to damage the skin. Season the inside of this envelope with salt and pepper. Splash with Cognac and port, and leave to marinate overnight.

Make a stuffing with the neck of pork, veal fillet, a few chicken livers, the goose or duck liver, and truffles. Mix everything together with 2 or 3 eggs.

Fill the duck envelope with this stuffing and then carefully sew it back up and tie it up like a sausage. Put in a roasting pan with some butter and cook in a hot oven—how long depends on the size of the bird, about an hour for a duck.

Refrigerate overnight.

(Over) Roger Garnier (left) and the apprentices at col de la Luère   157

DINDONNE RÔTIE AUX MARRONS

ROAST TURKEY WITH TRUFFLE AND CHESTNUTS

1 (6.5- TO 9-LB)
TURKEY
SALT
TRUFFLES
BUTTER
4.5 LB ARDÈCHE
CHESTNUTS

Salt the inside of the turkey. Slide under the skin of the breast and thighs slices of fresh truffle. Truss the bird and put it on to roast in a large cocotte with butter. Allow 15 minutes cooking for each pound.

When the turkey is well colored, start to baste regularly with a little water. Repeat a few times.

Split the skins of the chestnuts and put in a hot oven for 10 minutes. Take off the skins and put the chestnuts around the turkey for the last hour of cooking.

To get a tender flesh, joint the turkey 30 minutes before the end of the cooking. Put the pieces back in the cocotte with the chestnuts and the jus, and finish the cooking over a low flame in the corner of the stove.

♈ Red Bordeaux, Burgundy, Châteauneuf-du-Pape

DINDONNE TRUFFÉE POCHÉE

POACHED TRUFFLED TURKEY

1 (6.5-LB) TURKEY
TRUFFLES
SEA SALT
2.25 LB BEEF
1 VEAL HOCK
CARROTS
TURNIPS
LEEKS
1 STALK CELERY
PEPPER
MUSTARD
GHERKINS
MORELLO CHERRIES
    PRESERVED IN
    VINEGAR

Truffle a good white turkey as for *Dindonne Rôtie aux Marrons* (opposite). Truss and wrap in muslin. Put it on to cook in a large saucepan, covered in water. Salt with sea salt. Add the beef in pieces and the veal hock. At the first boiling, skim completely. Cook at a low simmer and allow 15 minutes for each pound.

After 30 minutes, add the carrots, the turnips, the leeks—cut short and trimmed—and the celery. Keep the cooking to a simmer. Check the seasoning.

Serve the turkey surrounded by its vegetables, with the beef and the veal hock. Do not forget to serve, at the same time, sea salt, mustard, gherkins, and sour Morello cherries.

It can be accompanied with a curried rice. You can also serve each guest with a cup of the stock, sieved first.

♟ Red Burgundy, red Bordeaux, red Hermitage

PERDREAUX, FAISANS, GRIVES, OU CAILLES RÔTIS

ROASTED PARTRIDGE, PHEASANT, THRUSH, OR QUAIL

All the feathered game birds are usually roasted. The most difficult thing is to get young birds, especially pheasant and partridges. Do not forget that these birds are all lean and need to be cooked with plenty of butter. La Mère—economy always first—would reproach us if we did not add enough butter.

1 PARTRIDGE, PHEASANT, THRUSH, OR QUAIL
SALT
PEPPER
STRIPS OF FATTY BACON
LEAN BACON LARDONS
BUTTER
COGNAC
½ GLASS WHITE WINE
GOOSE OR DUCK LIVER TRIMMINGS
MUSTARD
WHITE OF BREAD

Pluck and burn off the stubble properly on the bird; gut. Salt and pepper and put the liver back in the bird. Wrap in fatty bacon.

In an earthenware or cast-iron cocotte, just big enough to hold the bird, fry some lardons in butter. When they have colored, take out the lardons and put in their place the game bird. Add butter as necessary.

Deglaze the pan with a splash of Cognac and, at the moment of serving, the white wine to make the butter sing.

Take the liver out of the bird and crush with goose or duck liver trimmings, a little mustard, and Cognac, then spread over white bread croutons fried in butter.

We serve these game birds with straw potatoes, or a potato cake, and a salad of watercress.

FOR PHEASANTS AND PARTRIDGE: As soon as they have colored, put the cocotte in the oven to finish cooking.

FOR QUAILS AND THRUSHES: You can add a few grapes before the end of the cooking.

♀ Red Burgundy, red Hermitage, Châteauneuf-du-Pape

PERDREAUX AUX CHOUX

PARTRIDGE WITH CABBAGE

*Barding—laying on thin slices of bacon or pork fat—helps
the flesh of game birds retain its succulence.*

2 FIRM WHITE
    CABBAGES
SALT
1 OLDER PARTRIDGE
    OR 1 OLDER HEN
    PHEASANT
BUTTER
4.5 OZ LEAN BACON,
    SLICED
1 ONION
3 TO 4 CLOVES
2 YOUNG PARTRIDGES
STRIPS OF FATTY
    BACON

Cut the cabbages in quarters. Blanch in salted water and refresh
in cold water. Let them drain well.

To make the sauce, start to sauté the older partridge or the hen
pheasant in butter. When it is well colored, put it in the oven
for 10 minutes with slices of lean bacon. Put the cabbage in a
large cocotte with an onion studded with cloves. Lay on top the
partridge or hen pheasant and the slices of bacon. Close the
cocotte and cook in a gentle oven for an hour.

Meanwhile, prepare the young partridges, singe, and wrap
in the bacon. Roast them in a cocotte. Deglaze the cocotte
with water.

To serve, arrange the cabbage on a plate with the slices of bacon.
Carve the partridges in two and lay on top. Baste with the jus
from the other partridge or pheasant and serve on very hot
plates. The older partridge or pheasant can be eaten cold the
next day.

♈ Red Burgundy, red Bordeaux

FAISAN À LA FICELLE

STUFFED PHEASANT COOKED OVER VINE LEAVES

1 PHEASANT
FATTY BACON
1 YOUNG PHEASANT
SALT
PEPPER
1 GLASS PORT
BUTTER

Debone the older pheasant and chop the flesh with some bacon—about half as much. Add the pheasant liver and gizzard. Season with pepper, salt, and add the port. Mix the stuffing well.

Fill the young pheasant with this stuffing and sew up. Wrap in bacon.

Tie up the legs of the pheasant with strong string and suspend it over a good fire of vine clippings and twigs. Give the pheasant a push so it starts to swing. Baste often with melted butter. Give the pheasant a nudge every now and then, if it is not turning enough. Allow 90 minutes of cooking.

Cut the pheasant in four and serve the stuffing on each piece. Accompany with sautéed potatoes and an endive salad.

♟ Red Bordeaux, red Burgundy, red Hermitage

FAISAN EN COCOTTE

POT-ROAST PHEASANT

1 PHEASANT
SALT
PEPPER
2 TO 3 TABLESPOONS
   HEAVY CREAM
BACON
BUTTER
1 GLASS MADEIRA
1 GLASS WHITE WINE

After gutting and singeing the pheasant, salt and pepper the insides, and put in the stomach 2 or 3 spoons of cream. Wrap the bird in bacon and truss. Brown it in a cocotte with a good piece of butter.

When it is well colored, cover the cocotte and finish the cooking in the oven for 35 to 40 minutes, depending on the size and age of the pheasant.

Take out the pheasant and pour or skim off the fat from the cooking. Carve the bird into four and keep warm. Put the carcass back into the cocotte. Splash with Madeira and white wine. Adjust the seasoning and pour the sauce over the pheasant pieces.

You can serve this with straw potatoes, a puree of chestnuts, or mushrooms . . .

♟ Red Bordeaux, red Burgundy, Châteauneuf-du-Pape

FAISAN AU POMMARD

PHEASANT IN POMMARD

Pommard may be too expensive these days, but match the cooking wine with what you are drinking at the table.

1 PHEASANT
SALT
PEPPER
½ CUP BUTTER
1 LB SHELLED
   CHESTNUTS
1 BOTTLE POMMARD
   OR ANOTHER
   GOOD BURGUNDY
1 SHALLOT

Gut and singe a pheasant or—even better—a hen bird. Salt and pepper the inside and outside. Truss and color on all sides, in a cocotte, with a good piece of butter. Put in the oven for 10 minutes.

After this, put shelled chestnuts around the pheasant, reserving 5 for later. Add in almost a bottle of Pommard, to come halfway up the bird. Leave to cook for 25 to 30 minutes.

Take out of the oven, lift out the pheasant, and keep warm. In the casserole dish, squash and crush 5 chestnuts with the remaining butter.

Reduce the cooking jus, adding chopped shallot and, away from the flame, mix in the chestnut-butter mix.

Carve the pheasant and sieve the sauce over. Serve with the chestnuts as garnish.

♟ Pommard

BÉCASSE RÔTIE SUR CANAPÉ

ROAST WOODCOCK

We advise against hanging woodcock for too long. One week in the air—the cellar—seems sufficient to us. The first woodcock of the season, killed around All Saints Day, are the best, because they have not yet had to suffer the shortages of winter.

1 WOODCOCK
FATTY BACON
COGNAC
WHITE WINE
GOOSE OR DUCK
    LIVER
MUSTARD
SALT
PEPPER
WHITE OF BREAD
BUTTER

Wrap a fine woodcock in the fatty bacon. Put on to cook in an earthenware or cast-iron cocotte, without gutting—15 minutes on a high heat should be enough.

Carve the woodcock into four and put the broken bones back into the cocotte, wet with a little Cognac and white wine.

Take out the intestines, grind in a mortar, and push through a fine sieve. Mix with the liver, a little mustard, Cognac, salt, and pepper. Fry slices of bread in butter to make croutons.

Serve the quarters of woodcock basted in the jus with the croutons, without any other garnish.

♟ A grand Bordeaux, red Burgundy

RÔTIES DE BÉCASSES, DE GRIVES, OU D'ALOUETTES

ROAST WOODCOCK, THRUSH, OR LARK CANAPÉS

This recipe is less spectacular than serving the roasted birds whole, but it can be done ahead. And it is easier to eat, because there are no bones.

WOODCOCKS,
    THRUSH, OR LARKS
BUTTER
COGNAC
WHITE WINE
FOIE GRAS
MUSTARD
TRUFFLES
SALT
PEPPER
WHITE OF BREAD

Cook the game traditionally, which is to say in a cocotte with butter and then finished in the oven for bigger birds. Do not gut the woodcock. The birds should be lightly pink.

Take the birds out of the cocotte and make a jus by deglazing it with Cognac and white wine.

Debone the birds completely and grind the meat with a pestle and mortar or in an electric blender, with the intestines for woodcock (except the gizzard). Mix the flesh with foie gras, mustard, chopped truffle, Cognac, salt, and pepper. Spread on croutons made with the whites of bread fried in butter. Keep warm in an ovenproof dish 10 minutes before serving.

At the last moment, baste the canapés with the cooking jus.

♆ Grand Bordeaux, Burgundy

SALMIS DE BÉCASSES

WOODCOCK SALMIS

2 WOODCOCK
BUTTER
4.5 OZ MUSHROOMS
3.5 OZ TRUFFLES
1 SPOON MIREPOIX
1 GLASS COGNAC
2 GLASSES WHITE
    WINE
SALT
PEPPER
CORNSTARCH

In a cocotte, roast the woodcock (without gutting) with a good piece of butter and finish for 10 to 12 minutes in the oven. Meanwhile slice and sweat the mushrooms in butter in a pan.

Carve each bird into four and take off the skin. Put the pieces in a buttered frying pan, cover with the mushrooms and sliced truffles.

Warm through the carcasses in the cocotte along with any trimmings and the mirepoix. Wet with Cognac, white wine, and a little water, or—even better—game stock. Salt, pepper, and lightly bind with a little cornstarch. Add some butter and strain this sauce over the pieces of woodcock.

Make some canapés with the liver and the intestines.

♓ Bordeaux, red Burgundy

PIGEONNEAUX EN CRAPAUDINE

ROAST PIGEON, CROUCHING

The best way to conserve all the flavor of a pigeon is to roast it. Straw potatoes go very well with this pigeon.

1 YOUNG PIGEON
SALT
PEPPER
BUTTER
BREAD CRUMBS
1 HARD-BOILED EGG
WATERCRESS
SAUCE BÉARNAISE
    (PAGE 255)

Pull the legs of the pigeon into its stomach and split it from the stomach to the wing—this gives it the shape of a toad. Salt, pepper, and seal in the oven with a little butter. Take out of the oven and cover with fine bread crumbs. Baste with melted butter and cook for 10 minutes (bloody) or 20 minutes (well done) at the top of the oven.

At the moment of service, cover the eyes with small rounds of egg white with smaller slices of truffle for pupils.

Serve on a hot plate surrounded by watercress, with a *sauce béarnaise* to the side.

♓ All red wines

CAILLES AU NID

QUAILS IN THEIR NEST

If you cannot find wild birds, it is possible to buy free-range, but factory-farm birds should be avoided.

QUAILS
GODIVEAU STUFFING
  OR OTHER
  SAUSAGE MEAT
FRESH GOOSE OR
  DUCK LIVER
TRUFFLES
FATTY BACON
WHITE WINE
MADEIRA
SALT
PEPPER
HEAVY CREAM
BUTTER
CORNSTARCH
STRAW POTATOES
THIN PANCAKES
MUSHROOMS

Debone the quails. Keep the heads back for decoration. Use the bones and trimmings to make a strong stock.

Stuff the birds with the godiveau sausage meat, the liver, and chopped truffle. Fold over, roll into ballotines, and wrap around with bacon. Poach in the stock thinned with white wine and Madeira; salt and pepper.

Once poached, color the quails in the oven by taking off the bacon wrapping.

Reduce the cooking liquid, bind with cream and butter and, if needed, a little cornstarch.

Make up the straw potatoes into a nest big enough to take the quails and their garnish. The bed of the nest should be covered with very thin pancakes. Put the quails in and put their heads back on. Add some large dice of truffle and mushroom heads, sweated in butter.

Serve the sauce in a sauceboat to the side.

♈ Red Bordeaux, red Burgundy

PINTADEAUX RÔTIS

ROASTED GUINEA FOWL

If you cannot find small guinea fowl, you can substitute Cornish game hens.

1 GUINEA FOWL
   PER PERSON
SALT
PEPPER
BUTTER
LEAN BACON
COGNAC
½ GLASS WHITE WINE

Choose very small guinea fowl—not much bigger than a quail—salt and pepper, and wrap in the bacon. In a cocotte just big enough to contain them, warm some butter and blanch some lardons of bacon. When they are colored, take them out and put the guinea fowl in their place. Roast in the oven, turning often. That should take about 15 minutes.

Take out the birds and deglaze the cocotte with a splash of Cognac and the white wine. Check the seasoning.

Take off the bacon from around the guinea fowl. Cut the birds in half lengthwise and put them back into the cocotte, with the lardons, to color in their sauce.

Serve from their cooking cocotte. Accompany with straw potatoes.

♆ Red Burgundy, Bordeaux, Châteauneuf-du-Pape

GIGUE DE CHEVREUIL, DE CERFS, JAMBON DE SANGLIER GRAND VENEUR

HAUNCH OF VENISON, ROE DEER, WILD BOAR

GAME MEAT
CARROTS
ONIONS
PEPPERCORNS
PARSLEY
BOUQUET GARNI
1 BOTTLE WHITE
   BURGUNDY
FATTY BACON
SAUCE POIVRADE
   (PAGE 173
SALT
CORNSTARCH
HEAVY CREAM

Marinate the meat—venison or boar—for 48 hours with carrots, onions, peppercorns, parsley, and a bouquet garni, covered with good, white Burgundy.

Drain and wipe dry the meat and wrap in fatty bacon. Use marinade to braise on top of the oven. Then continue to cook in the oven, basting from time to time with a little of the marinade.

With the bones and the trimmings from the meat, make a *sauce poivrade*, to which you add the cooking juices from the meat. Adjust the seasoning of the sauce and bind with a little cornstarch. At the last moment add in a little heavy cream.

Carve the meat and serve the sauce, very hot, to the side. Accompany with a puree of chestnuts.

♉ Grand Bordeaux, grand Burgundy

MARINADE DE LA MÈRE BRAZIER

MÈRE BRAZIER'S MARINADE FOR ALL GAME

CARROTS
ONIONS
SHALLOTS
PARSLEY
THYME
BAY LEAF
1 STALK CELERY
RED OR WHITE WINE
1 GLASS VINEGAR
OLIVE OIL
SALT
PEPPERCORNS
CLOVES

Chop the carrots, onions, and shallots. Put half of them, along with half the parsley, thyme, bay, celery in a terrine.

Place the meats to marinate on top and cover with the rest of the vegetables and aromatics. Cover with red or white wine, depending on the dish, and a glass of vinegar, a few spoons of olive oil, salt, peppercorns, and cloves. Keep in the open air, turning the pieces of meat a few times.

For bigger pieces, you can cook the marinade, which is to say color the vegetables and aromatics in olive oil. Add the wine and vinegar and cook for 30 minutes. Leave to cool completely before pouring over the pieces of meat to marinate.

SAUCE MOSCOVITE POUR VENAISON

MUSCOVITE SAUCE FOR VENISON

2 CUPS SAUCE
   POIVRADE
   (OPPOSITE)
VENISON STOCK
SCANT ½ CUP
   MALAGA SWEET
   WINE
4 TABLESPOONS
   JUNIPER BERRIES
4 TABLESPOONS
   ALMONDS
4 TABLESPOONS
   CURRANTS

This sauce is based on sauce poivrade, *destined to go with venison, boar, and other meaty game.*

To the *sauce poivrade*, add the venison stock, Malaga sweet wine, juniper berries—infused in ⅓ cup hot water, as for a tea, for 10 minutes—roasted and peeled almonds, currants—soaked so they are full and swollen. Warm without boiling.

SAUCE POIVRADE POUR GIBIER

POIVRADE SAUCE FOR GAME

This sauce is used to make Sauce Grand Veneur, *achieved by introducing half a glass of the blood of the animal. Mix the blood with a little marinade. Allow it to cook gently without boiling for a few minutes. Sieve through a muslin cloth. If there is no blood, it is* sauce poivrade.

4 CARROTS

3 SHALLOTS

PARSLEY

THYME

BAY LEAF

OLIVE OIL

2 LB GAME
   TRIMMINGS

1¼ CUPS WINE
   VINEGAR

SCANT CUP WHITE
   WINE

2 QUARTS GAME
   STOCK

2 PINTS MARINADE DE
   LA MÈRE BRAZIER
   (OPPOSITE)

12 PEPPERCORNS

BUTTER (OPTIONAL)

Make a mirepoix of carrots, shallots, parsley stalks, thyme, a bay leaf. Warm through in olive oil with the trimmings from the game.

Once the meats have colored, drain off the oil. Wet with the wine vinegar and white wine, and reduce completely.

Add game stock, made using bones, and the marinade. Cook slowly in the oven, covered, for 3 hours.

Add crushed peppercorns and cook for another 40 minutes, straining completely. Check the seasoning.

You can add, at the last moment, a piece of butter to make the sauce more velvety and supple.

♇ Red Burgundy

RÂBLE DE LIÈVRE OU SELLE DE CHEVREUIL SAUPIQUET

SADDLE OF HARE OR VENISON, SAUCE SAUPIQUET

1 SADDLE OF HARE
 (OR SADDLE OF
 VENISON)
MARINADE DE LA
 MÈRE BRAZIER
 (PAGE 172)
FATTY BACON
1 ONION
BUTTER
SALT
PEPPER
BLOOD OF THE HARE
1 GLASS COGNAC
¼ CUP DICED
 SHALLOTS
HAM
1 CLOVE GARLIC
THYME
BAY LEAF

Marinate the saddle for 24 hours.

Take off the thin layer of skin that encases the saddle. Make some cuts in the flesh and insert small cubes of fatty bacon. Put on to roast in a cocotte with a chopped onion and a little butter; salt and pepper. The meat should stay slightly pink.

Blend in a mixer the hare's liver with the blood (if you have it) and a small glass of Cognac.

Sweat diced shallots and ham in butter. Add the minced garlic and wet with 1 pint of the marinade. Add thyme and bay, and leave to reduce by two-thirds.

Sieve this sauce into a new saucepan and bring to a boil. At the last minute whisk in the blood and liver to thicken.

Carve the saddle lengthwise and serve the sauce to the side. Accompany with whole or pureed chestnuts.

♉ Grand red Bordeaux

LIÈVRE À LA CRÈME

HARE IN CREAM

1 (6- TO 7-LB) HARE
WHITE WINE
SALT
PEPPERCORNS
BOUQUET GARNI
1 CARROT
1 ONION
1 GLASS COGNAC
5 OZ BACON
BUTTER
1 SHALLOT
1 SPOON FLOUR
2.25 PINTS HEAVY
   CREAM
MUSHROOMS
CAYENNE PEPPER
CORNSTARCH

If the hare gets too dry in the cooking, add some of the marinade.

Cut up the hare and marinate in a terrine; it needs to be covered with a good, aged white wine—a Burgundy works well. Add salt, peppercorns, the bouquet garni, a carrot cut in four, chopped onion, and Cognac. Leave out in the open and turn the pieces of hare a few times.

Drain the hare and wipe dry. In a large cocotte, warm bacon lardons in butter. Once they color take them out and keep ready.

Color the piece of hare in the same cocotte, with a diced shallot. Sprinkle over the flour, brown a little, then cover and leave to cook very slowly for about 2 hours.

When the hare is nearly cooked, add the fresh cream and let it simmer to the end of the cooking.

Take out the pieces of hare, arrange them on a plate with the lardons and some mushrooms sweated in butter.

Check the seasoning of the sauce, adding a little cayenne pepper. If necessary, bind with a little cornstarch. Pour the sauce through a sieve over the hare. Can be served with curried rice.

♀ Red Burgundy, red Bordeaux, red Hermitage

CIVET DE LIÈVRE OU DE LAPIN

HARE OR RABBIT STEW

Depending on the size of the hare or rabbit, the number of chopped pieces will vary from six to nine.

1 YOUNG HARE OR
  RABBIT
SALT
PEPPERCORNS
1 CARROT
1 SHALLOT
BOUQUET GARNI
PARSLEY
1 GLASS COGNAC
ROUGH RED WINE
1 SPOON OLIVE OIL
5 OZ LEAN BACON
  LARDONS
3 TO 4 SPOONS
  FLOUR
SMALL ONIONS
  (OPTIONAL)
MUSHROOMS
  (OPTIONAL)
BUTTER
CROUTONS

Keep the blood of the hare (if you have it) and gut the animal. Cut the hare into pieces and put them in a terrine with salt, peppercorns, a carrot cut in four, a chopped shallot, a bouquet garni, some parsley stalks. Wet with the Cognac and cover with a good, rough red wine—Bordeaux or Burgundy. Add the olive oil and leave to marinate for 1 or more days.

Take out the pieces and sieve the marinade.

In a large *coquille* (cocotte), warm the bacon lardons. When they are colored, take them out and keep them. Warm the vegetables from the marinade and then the pieces of hare. Cook the vegetables hard for a few minutes, then the pieces of hare, then sprinkle on the flour, and wet with all of the marinade. Leave to simmer slowly for at least 2 hours, depending on the age of the hare.

Take each piece of hare out with a fork and place in a table cocotte. Adjust the seasoning of the sauce, which should be noticeable, but not too much. Thicken the sauce by adding the blood from the animal, whipping vigorously. At the last moment, add a good piece of butter and sieve the sauce over the pieces of hare and the lardons. You can also add small onions or the heads of small mushrooms, cooked in butter.

Serve with croutons cut into triangles and dipped in chopped parsley at the tip. Accompany with steamed potatoes or fresh noodles.

♈ Grand Bordeaux, grand Burgundy

HURE DE MARCASSIN

BOAR'S HEAD

1 HEAD OF
  YOUNG BOAR
SALT
PEPPER
SALTPETER
SPICES (PEPPER,
  CLOVES, NUTMEG,
  CINNAMON)
SHALLOTS
PARSLEY
WHITE WINE
9 OZ VEAL
9 OZ PORK
2 EGGS
TRUFFLES
GOOSE OR DUCK
  LIVER (OPTIONAL)
ONIONS
CARROTS
BOUQUET GARNI
BUTTER
SAUCE TARTARE
  (PAGE 263)

Broil or singe the bristles off the head of a young boar. Wash carefully in boiling water. There must be no hairs left. Drain and debone the head completely. Lay the meat out flat and season with salt, pepper, saltpeter, spices, diced shallots, and parsley. Splash over the white wine and leave to marinate for 24 hours.

Make a stuffing with the veal meat and neck of pork. Chop finely, add the eggs, chopped shallots—sweated in butter—chopped truffle, and a little goose liver, if you have it.

Put the stuffing in the center of the head and sew up to give the head its original shape.

Wrap in a linen cloth, tie up, and put on to cook in a marmite with salt, pepper, onions, carrots, the bouquet garni, and the bones from the head. You can tell that it is cooked when a needle slips easily into the meat. Leave the head in the cooking liquid until it has cooled completely.

Serve to the side a good *sauce tartare*.

♆ Alsace, Pouilly-Fumé

LES VIANDES
MEAT

ÉPAULE DE MOUTON BOULANGÈRE

SHOULDER OF MUTTON BOULANGÈRE

A leg can be cooked in the same way. Mutton is hard to find, but a late-season, over-wintered, larger lamb may be used instead.

1 SHOULDER OF MUTTON
BUTTER
YELLOW WAXY POTATOES
ONION
SALT
PEPPER
SPRIG OF THYME

Debone the shoulder—take off all the bones. We recommend keeping it flat, not rolled.

Put some butter in a roasting dish, and put in some yellow potatoes—cut into rounds, a little thick— along with a chopped onion. Salt, pepper, and add the thyme. Put the mutton on top and slide into a hot oven. Allow 15 minutes per pound for *saignant*—pink.

When the shoulder is cooked, take it out and moisten the pan with a little water to make a jus.

Carve the shoulder and put back on the potatoes. Serve in its cooking dish, without any other garnish.

🍷 Beaujolais, Côte-Rôtie

BARON D'AGNEAU

ROAST BARON OF LAMB

The baron of lamb, which comprises the two gigots (legs) and the saddle, presumes a number of important guests. On the other hand, we need a few ideas to be able to deliver a perfect execution of this imposing piece. Nevertheless, guests will be impressed when presented with a baron, and it should be carved in front of them.

BARON OF LAMB
GARLIC
BUTTER
SALT
PEPPER

Rub the baron lightly with garlic. The cooking is in the oven with butter, salt, and pepper. We serve a baron lightly *saignant*—pink.

All seasonal vegetables go well.

🍷 Beaujolais, light Burgundy

CARRÉ D'AGNEAU GRILLÉ

GRILLED WHOLE RACK OF LAMB

A rack of lamb ought to be treated as one piece and comprises nine cutlets.

1 WHOLE RACK
OF LAMB
SALT
PEPPER
OIL

Trim the rack just as you would cutlets. Debone the back chine and take off completely, to make it easier to carve. Scrape the sleeves of the cutlet down to ¾ inch. Take off the skin that covers the meat. Salt, pepper, wipe with oil, and cook under a broiler, at the top of a hot oven, or grill over charcoal. Baste often. Do not overcook—it should be lightly *saignant*—pink.

Carve in front of the guests. Accompany with seasonal vegetables, Provençal tomatoes, or potatoes.

Ⴗ Côte-Rôtie, red Hermitage

NAVARIN DE MOUTON (RAGOÛT)

NAVARIN OF LAMB (STEW)

When shopping, choose firm turnips, unwrinkled and unmarked. Avoid those that are too big, as they have a tendency to be fibrous.

2 LB LAMB OR
MUTTON
BUTTER
2 SPOONS FLOUR
2 OR 3 CLOVES
GARLIC
BOUQUET GARNI
SALT
PEPPER
2 SPOONS TOMATO
PUREE
SMALL ONIONS
CARROTS
TURNIPS
POTATOES

Cut into pieces the mutton or lamb—shoulder, breast, or collar. Put in a cocotte with a little butter and let brown. Add the flour and leave to color, then add peeled garlic, the bouquet garni, salt, pepper, and the tomato puree, and cover with water or stock. Cover and cook on the stovetop for an hour or so, depending on the quality of the meat.

Add in the small onions, carrots, turnips—chopped into small pieces and browned in butter. Put in some potatoes cut into big dice. Finish the cooking, which in all should take 90 minutes to 2 hours.

Skim or pour off the fat from the sauce and serve on hot plates.

Ⴗ Côtes-du-Rhône, light Beaujolais nouveau

GIGOT DE MOUTON BRAISÉ À LA LYONNAISE

BRAISED LEG OF MUTTON LYONNAISE

1 BONE-IN LEG OF
  LAMB OR MUTTON
1 CLOVE GARLIC
1 ONION
CARROTS
DRY WHITF WINE
2 SPOONS TOMATO
  PUREE
SALT
PEPPER
30 SMALL ONIONS
BUTTER

Rub a well-rounded and fleshy leg of lamb or mutton with garlic. Brown in a casserole with a chopped onion and diced carrots.

Moisten with some dry white wine. Add the tomato puree; salt, pepper. Cover and cook slowly in the oven for 5 hours.

Warm the small onions in a pan in butter. When they are well colored, cover and let cook in their own steam. These onions will be the garnish—you may, of course, have other garnishes.

When the lamb is well cooked, serve using a spoon, because it will not be possible to cut with a knife.

Degrease the cooking juices and serve very hot.

♀ Beaujolais, Côtes-du-Rhône

SELLE D'AGNEAU RÔTIE

ROAST SADDLE OF LAMB

The saddle comprises the two loins and the rump. The difficulty is in the carving of a saddle, which must be done at the table. You need a long enough knife, with a very sharp, thin blade. Cut both sides of the saddle lengthwise in thin slices, just to the bone.

1 SADDLE OF LAMB
BUTTER
SALT
PEPPER

Rub the saddle all over with butter. Roast in a medium oven slightly longer than for a leg of lamb—about 20 minutes per pound, depending how thick it is.

When it is cooked, salt and pepper. Carve the meat. Make a jus by deglazing the roasting pan with a little water. Serve the jus to the side.

You can accompany this meat with a *Gratin Dauphinois* (page 77) or any other spring vegetables.

♀ Light Bordeaux, Burgundy, Hermitage

GIGOT D'AGNEAU À LA BROCHE

SPIT-ROAST LEG OF LAMB

Choose a well-rounded leg. Ask the butcher to take the bone out, which makes it easier to carve. Some people put the lamb in a cold oven—a mistake, because it stops the meat from sealing. Above all, never roast a gigot ahead of time. It should be enough to put it on when the guests are drinking their aperitifs.

1 LEG OF LAMB
1 CLOVE GARLIC
OLIVE OIL
SALT
PEPPER

Lightly rub over the leg of lamb with garlic. We don't advise sticking the cloves of garlic into the meat, because some people are afraid of the smell.

Wrap the tail and the "mouse" in aluminum foil. Wipe with olive oil.

Heat the broiler or the oven. Allow about 15 minutes cooking per pound.

Baste often and, when cooked, salt and pepper the whole piece.

To carve, start at the thin end and cut lengthwise.

Serve on hot plates, accompanied with seasonal vegetables, fried potatoes, watercress salad . . .

♀ Beaujolais, Côte-Rôtie, red Hermitage

BOEUF BOURGUIGNON

BEEF BURGUNDY

1 LB BEEF CHUCK OR
   TOP ROUND
LARD OR OIL
6 SMALL ONIONS
1 SPOON FLOUR
1 CLOVE GARLIC
1 BOTTLE RED WINE
1 SPOON TOMATO
   PUREE
BOUQUET GARNI
STREAKY BACON
SALT
PEPPER
MUSHROOMS
PARSLEY

Choose meat that is not too lean. Cut into large cubes and brown in lard or oil in a pan over a high heat.

Add the small onions, brown them. Add the flour, let cook for a minute.

Add the garlic and cover with red wine. Add the tomato puree, bouquet garni, and some diced, sweated, streaky bacon cut into small lardons; salt and pepper. Cover and cook slowly for about 2 hours.

Add in raw mushrooms and cook on for another 15 minutes.

Serve hot, scattered with chopped parsley. Serve with a puree of potatoes or fresh noodles.

℞ Light red Burgundy, red Hermitage

FILET DE CHAROLAIS ROSSINI

FILLET STEAK ROSSINI

This dish is simple enough, but must be executed at the last minute. The recipe uses foie gras naturel (terrine), but this dish can also be served with foie gras cooked in the pan.

1 CHAROLAIS FILLET
   STEAK PER PERSON
BUTTER
SALT
PEPPER
1 SHALLOT
1 GLASS PORT
FOIE GRAS AU
   NATUREL (PAGE 62)
TRUFFLE

Cook the steaks in a pan in a good piece of butter. Keep the cooking rare or well done according to each guest's taste. Salt and pepper. Take out the steaks and keep warm.

Fry a finely chopped shallot until it just starts to whiten. Deglaze with a good glass of port.

On each piece of meat, lay a slice of foie gras, and a slice of truffle.

At the last moment, add a nut of butter to the boiling sauce. Whisk vigorously for a few seconds. It should be quite strong. Pour over the steaks.

℞ Red Bordeaux

BOEUF MODE

BRAISED BEEF

To make this dish successfully, you need at least two pounds of beef. Ask the butcher to bard it with bacon or fat. Also ask him to bone the trotter. Literally, the recipe asks for pork rinds but a small, thin belly works, too.

1 (2-LB) PIECE OF BEEF
LARD
WHITE WINE
1 VEAL TROTTER
2 PORK CHEEKS
SALT
PEPPER
BOUQUET GARNI
30 SMALL ONIONS
CARROTS

Warm the beef through in lard in a large casserole, to seal. Let it color well on all sides.

Cover the meat with half water and half white wine.

Add the veal trotter—deboned—and the pork rinds. Season with salt, pepper, and the bouquet garni. Cover and leave to cook for an hour.

Add the onions and enough carrots—chopped into rounds—to make a portion. Leave to cook for another 90 minutes.

Degrease the sauce, check the seasoning, and serve very hot, with the carrots, taking care to chop the trotter into small pieces.

Can equally be served cold.

♆ Beaujolais, Côtes-du-Rhône

BOEUF SAUTÉ À LA LYONNAISE

BEEF LYONNAISE

This recipe is ideally for the leftovers from a pot au feu *or a braise of beef.*

2 OR 3 ONIONS
BUTTER
COOKED BEEF
SALT
PEPPER
PARSLEY

Chop 2 or 3 onions, depending on the quantity of meat. Warm through, in a pan, in some butter.

Slice the beef thinly and, in another pan, warm through in butter.

Bring the onions and the meat together and sauté everything together, seasoning with salt and pepper.

Serve with some chopped parsley and sautéed potatoes.

♆ Coteaux-du-Lyonnais

BOULETTES DE BOEUF AU SANCERRE

BEEF MEATBALLS IN SANCERRE

7 OZ LEAN BEEF
14 OZ NECK OF PORK
3.5 OZ VEAL
1 ONION
1 SHALLOT
PARSLEY
SALT
PEPPER
FLOUR
LEAN BACON FAT
BUTTER
2 GLASSES RED
  SANCERRE WINE
1 BOUQUET GARNI

Chop all the meats together with the onion, shallot, and a little parsley. Season with salt and pepper and mix well. Form into little balls about the size of an egg and roll them in flour.

Warm the bacon fat and some butter in a cocotte. Put in the balls and wet with red Sancerre and a glass of water. Add the bouquet garni and leave to bubble for about an hour.

Serve with rice, fresh noodles, or a puree of potatoes.

♆ Red Sancerre

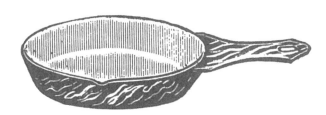

ENTRECÔTES À LA BORDELAISE

STEAK BORDELAISE

Turn the steaks in the pan when drops of blood rise to the surfaces that have not yet cooked.

MINUTE STEAKS
1 OR 2 SHALLOTS
2 TO 3 PINCHES
   FLOUR
1 GLASS RED
   BORDEAUX
SALT
PEPPER
BEEF BONE MARROW
PARSLEY

Cook the steaks in a pan with butter, keeping them slightly pink or *saignant*. Take them out of the pan and keep warm.

In the pan, add finely chopped shallots and cook for a few minutes, then add the flour. Wet with the Bordeaux. Salt, pepper, and add the beef bone marrow, cut into rounds. Let it melt a little in the sauce.

Put the steaks on hot plates, pour over the sauce, scatter over some chopped parsley, and decorate each steak with a round of bone marrow.

Can be served with fries or fresh noodles.

♉ Light red Bordeaux

GOULASCH DE BOEUF AU RIZ

BEEF GOULASH WITH RICE

The origin of goulash is Hungarian. It is the Magyar name for the cattle herders—golyas.

1.25 LB SHIN, SHANK,
   OR BEEF ROUND
FATTY BACON
2 ONIONS
1 BELL PEPPER
¼ CUP BUTTER
SALT
PEPPER
PAPRIKA

Chop the meat into large dice and the fatty bacon into little lardons. Chop very finely the onions and bell pepper.

Put the butter in a cocotte, then a layer of lardons, then a layer of beef, salt, pepper, and paprika; cover with a layer of onions and bell pepper. Put over another layer of beef, salt, pepper, paprika, and the rest of the onions and peppers. Moisten with 2 glasses of water and cover. Leave to cook on stove for 3 hours, slowly.

Serve very hot with a plate of rice.

♉ A rough red

BLANQUETTE DE VEAU

BLANQUETTE OF VEAL

*Young veal, raised under its mother, is always of
excellent quality.*

1.25 LB BREAST AND
   SHOULDER OF VEAL
SMALL ONIONS
1 CARROT
BOUQUET GARNI
SALT
PEPPER
BEURRE MANIÉ
   (PAGE 254)
HEAVY CREAM
EGG YOLKS
MUSHROOMS
GHERKINS

Cut the meat into bite-size pieces. Put them in a large cocotte and
wash in cold water. Put on to cook, and, as soon as it starts to
boil, skim off any froth completely.

Add a few small onions, the carrot split in four, the bouquet
garni, salt, and pepper, and leave to cook gently for 90 minutes,
depending on the quantity of meat.

Drain and reserve the cooking liquid. Bind the latter with the
beurre manié and let this sauce cook for 15 minutes.

Mix together in a new bowl, a few spoons of cream and 1
or 2 egg yolks, salt, and pepper. Whisk vigorously into the
sauce. Add in some cooked sliced mushrooms, and 1 or 2
chopped gherkins.

Serve the veal very hot on hot plates with the sauce. This is
usually accompanied with rice—plain or seasoned with curry.

♀ Light red

LA MÈRE'S
CLASSIC MENU No.5

Soufflé de Saumon
Salmon Soufflé (page 50)

◆

Quenelles au Gratin
Quenelle Gratin

◆

Filet de Charolais Rossini
Fillet Steak Rossini (page 184)

◆

Fromages de Saison
Seasonal Cheeses

◆

Sorbets aux Fruits
Fruit Sorbet (page 239)

◆

Galette Bressane
Bresse Galette (page 248)

GRENADINS DE VEAU

VEAL GRENADIERS

A grenadier is a thick, straight veal cutlet. Ask your butcher to slip bacon pieces into the flesh of the veal.

1 GRENADIER PER
  PERSON
BUTTER
BACON
ONION
CARROT
STOCK
BOUQUET GARNI
SALT
PEPPER
CORNSTARCH

Put the veal in a roasting pan with butter and bacon. Warm through with chopped onion and carrot. Wet with stock or water. Add the bouquet garni. Salt, pepper, and braise in the oven, basting often.

Present the grenadiers on a plate. Thicken the jus with a little cornstarch diluted in water. Check the seasoning and sieve the jus over the veal.

Serve on very hot plates with seasonal vegetables or fresh noodles.

♀ Light red

ESCALOPES PANÉES

VEAL SCALLOPS IN BREAD CRUMBS

It is not necessary to use veal tenderloin for these scallops, the "baker's nut" works just as well—taken from the front of the thigh and traditionally used to fill a baker's vol-au-vents, or for roasts.

1 VEAL SCALLOP
  PER PERSON
SALT
PEPPER
FLOUR
1 EGG
OIL
BREAD CRUMBS
BUTTER

Flatten the scallops on a board with the help of the side of a big knife. Salt, pepper, flour, and dip in a mix of a beaten egg, a spoon of water, one of oil, a pinch of salt, and one of pepper—and then dredge through the bread crumbs. Fry in butter in a thick-bottomed pan or—better still—in a cast-iron pan. Cook gently.

Can be served in different ways: garnished with a round of lemon, topped with an anchovy fillet. With a tomato *concasse*, sautéed in butter. With fresh noodles. With leaf spinach. With artichoke hearts *à la Clamart* (filled with peas).

♀ Light red

ESCALOPES DE VEAU PETRONIANA

VEAL PETRONIANA

1 VEAL SCALLOP
  PER PERSON
SALT
PEPPER
BUTTER
PROSCIUTTO
GRUYÈRE CHEESE

Fry the scallops in butter in a small frying pan. Season with salt and pepper.

Halfway through the cooking, take them out and put them in a buttered gratin dish. Cover each scallop with a slice of prosciutto and some thin slices of Gruyère cheese.

Pass it through a very hot oven for a few minutes to melt and gratinate the cheese.

Accompany with spaghetti or rice.

♈ Beaujolais, red Hermitage

CÔTES DE VEAU POJARSKI

VEAL POJARSKI

Pojarski was a Russian innkeeper who performed this difficult trick of re-forming the veal on its bones for Tsar Nicholas II at the start of the nineteenth century.

1 VEAL CUTLET
  PER PERSON
BUTTER
BREAD CRUMBS
MILK
SALT
PEPPER

Take the cutlets off the bones and trim off any nerves. Keep the bones. Chop the cutlet and mix with a quarter of its weight of butter—mixed with bread crumbs soaked in milk and pressed dry. Salt, pepper, and, with this hash, cook the cutlets like patties in butter in a frying pan, browning both sides. Turn the cutlets carefully with a spatula because they are very fragile.

Serve with seasonal vegetables or fresh noodles.

♈ Light red

PAUPIETTES DE VEAU BRAISÉES

BRAISED VEAL ROLLS

The veal olive is one of those slow-cooked dishes that allows many variations of the stuffing ... with cabbage, with fish.

1 THIN VEAL SCALLOP
   PER PERSON
SALT
PEPPER
SLICE OF
   COOKED HAM
BUTTER
1 ONION
1 CARROT

Take one side of the veal olive and flatten on a board. Salt lightly and pepper, then cover with half a thin slice of cooked ham. Roll up and tie with string.

In a cocotte, put some butter, a chopped onion, and chopped carrot, and warm through the olives with the vegetables. When everything is well colored, wet with water and cook in the oven, basting often to braise it well—allow about an hour.

Arrange the olives on a plate, taking off the string. Check the seasoning of the jus and pour over the veal.

Serve with seasonal vegetables or with fresh noodles.

🍷 Red

POITRINE DE VEAU FARCIE

STUFFED BREAST OF VEAL

This dish can only be made for a number of important guests.

½ BREAST OF VEAL
1 SHALLOT
BUTTER
FINES HERBES
SAUSAGE MEAT
1 EGG
SALT
PEPPER
ONIONS
CARROTS
STOCK

Take the meat off the bones and split down the middle lengthwise. In the middle, create a kind of pocket.

Fry the chopped shallot in butter, add in the diced *fines herbes*, and take off the heat. Mix with the sausage meat, egg, salt, and pepper. Fill the pocket.

Sew the breast up carefully and braise with chopped onions and carrots. Brown the whole piece and wet with stock or water. Cover the cocotte and cook in the oven for at least 2 hours.

To serve, cut into slices and pour the jus on top. Accompany with seasonal vegetables. Can equally be eaten cold.

🍷 Red

MÉDALLIONS DE VEAU
À LA PROVENÇALE

VEAL MEDALLIONS PROVENÇAL

1 VEAL TENDERLOIN
OLIVE OIL
SMOKED BACON
KIDNEYS
SALT
PEPPER
THYME

Cut the fillet of veal into medallions and brown in the olive oil. Lift out the medallions and wrap in the smoked bacon.

Cut the kidneys into rounds and warm them in the same pan as the medallions.

Skewer alternately the kidney rounds and medallions. Salt, pepper, and sprinkle with thyme. Paint with oil and charcoal-grill.

Serve with Provençal tomatoes and sautéed or broiled mushrooms.

♈ Rosé de Provence

SAUTÉ DE VEAU MARENGO

VEAL MARENGO

Napoleon Bonaparte defeated the Austrians at the battle of Marengo, in Italy, on June 14, 1800.

1 SHOULDER OF VEAL
OIL
BUTTER
1 ONION
1 SPOON FLOUR
1 CLOVE GARLIC
2 GLASSES DRY WHITE
  WINE
2 SPOONS TOMATO
  PUREE
SALT
PEPPER
MUSHROOMS
PARSLEY
CROUTONS

Cut the veal into large pieces. Warm in a cocotte oil and butter. Brown the veal pieces.

Add finely chopped onion and the flour, and leave to brown a few moments. Add crushed garlic and wet with the dry white wine and tomato puree. Salt, pepper, and leave to cook slowly for an hour in the covered cocotte.

Add in some raw mushrooms, leave to cook about another 10 minutes.

Degrease the sauce carefully. Serve very hot with chopped parsley and small croutons fried in butter.

Can be accompanied by seasonal vegetables or fresh noodles.

♈ Light red

TENDRONS DE VEAU

VEAL TENDRONS

The tendron, a barded and unctuous cut, is situated near the thorax, at the top of the breast.

BREAST OF VEAL
ONIONS
CARROTS
BUTTER
STOCK
SALT
PEPPER
TURNIPS
CELERY

Cut the breast lengthwise into strips 2 fingers wide. Put in a cocotte with diced onions, carrots, and butter. Brown it well.

Cover to three-quarters full with stock or water. Salt, pepper, and bring to a boil, then put in a medium oven, uncovered and basting often, for 2 hours.

In an ovenproof frying pan, warm through in butter some onions, carrots, turnips, and chopped celery. Cover and leave to steam in the oven for 20 minutes.

Ten minutes before the veal is ready, add the vegetables to the meat and leave to cook together.

To serve, degrease the jus and present very hot.

Accompany with seasonal vegetables.

♈ Côtes-du-Rhône

CÔTES DE VEAU BONNE FEMME

VEAL CUTLETS BONNE FEMME

12 SMALL ONIONS
LEAN BACON
BUTTER
1 THICK VEAL CUTLET
   PER PERSON
PEPPER
SALT
FLOUR
MUSHROOMS
1 GLASS DRY
   WHITE WINE
STOCK

In a cocotte warm a dozen small onions and some lardons in butter. When they are well colored, take them out and replace them in the pan with peppered, salted, and floured veal cutlets. Brown on both sides.

Put the onions and lardons back in, along with some sliced mushrooms, cooked in butter. Wet with wine and a little stock. Cover and leave to cook for 30 minutes more.

Serve very hot with its sauce, which should not be too wet—reduce it as much as you need.

Serve with spinach leaves or a mix of seasonal vegetables.

♈ Rosé, light red

CÔTES DE VEAU À LA CRÈME

VEAL CUTLETS IN CREAM

Cook the cutlets over a low flame to keep them tender.

SALT
PEPPER
FLOUR
1 THICK VEAL CUTLET
   PER PERSON
1 TO 2 SHALLOTS
BUTTER
HEAVY CREAM
MUSHROOMS
LEMON

Salt, pepper, and flour the cutlets.

In a thick-bottomed pan, fry 1 or 2 finely chopped shallots in butter. As soon as they whiten, take them out and replace them with the cutlets. Brown on both sides. Cover the pan and let cook gently for 15 minutes.

Put the shallots back in the pan with a few spoons of heavy cream to get a thick sauce. Add a few quartered mushrooms. Check the seasoning and allow to bubble for 4 to 5 minutes.

Add a squeeze of lemon and serve very hot.

Usually served with rice.

♈ Light white, rosé

BAECKEOFE

ALSACE BAKER'S PIE

This dish from Alsace was, in the second half of the nineteenth century, entrusted to the baker's oven, the baeckeofe. *Quantities are enough to fill your cocotte.*

FRESH PORK
MUTTON
DRY WHITE RIESLING
 WINE
POTATOES
ONIONS
THYME
BAY LEAF
SALT
PEPPER
BUTTER

Chop up into big pieces an equal quantity of pork and mutton—preferably a cut close to the shoulder. Leave to marinate the night before in white wine, Riesling preferably.

In a large cocotte, earthenware if possible, put a layer of potatoes cut into large rounds. Put a few pieces of meat on top. Cover with another layer of potatoes and chopped onions, a little thyme, and a bay leaf. Alternate layers of meat and vegetables, ending with a layer of potato.

Salt, pepper, and moisten with the marinade, enough to cover the potatoes completely. Scatter over some nuts of butter. Start it on top of the oven, and then cover, and put in a gentle oven for 2 hours. Serve very hot in its cooking dish.

♈ Riesling or another Alsace wine

CÔTES DE PORC GRAND-MÈRE

GRANDMOTHER'S PORK CHOPS

1 PORK CHOP PER
 PERSON
BUTTER
1 ONION
1 EGG
SALT
PEPPER
CAUL FAT

Debone the pork chops and chop the meat. Add ½ cup butter for each pound of meat, plus a chopped onion, softened already in butter, and an egg. Salt, pepper, and mix this hash well.

Re-form the meat back around the bones. Wrap up in caul to hold. Broil slowly, basting with melted butter.

Shape like a crown. Serve with a puree of potatoes.

♈ All red wines

CARRÉ DE PORC À LA PAYSANNE

COUNTRY LOIN OF ROAST PORK AND POTATOES

A supremely efficient one-dish meal, with everything cooked in a single pot. You can add other vegetables as well as potatoes and, if it is looking a bit too dry, a glass of white wine—ideally the same as the one you will be serving. At the restaurant it would always have been a Rhône or a Beaujolais. The cooking time really depends on the size of your dish, and therefore your joint, but if it is not too big you can add the vegetables early.

1 LOIN OF PORK
BUTTER
2.5 LB POTATOES
2 OR 3 ONIONS
SALT
PEPPER
PARSLEY

Put a loin of pork, trimmed by the butcher, into the oven to roast. Roast preferably in an earthenware dish for about 20 minutes per pound, with a little butter, in a hot oven so it takes well.

Halfway through the cooking, surround the loin with potatoes, chopped into quarters. Add chopped onions, sautéed in butter. Salt and pepper. Baste the potatoes often with the pork jus. The pork should be well cooked.

Serve in its cooking dish, scattered with chopped parsley.

♀ Beaujolais, Côte-Rôtie, red Hermitage

CHOUCROUTE À L'ALSACIENNE

ALSACE CHOUCROUTE

Montbéliard are sausages smoked over sawdust from Franche-Comté, next to Alsace. Serve at the same time as the choucroute a small glass of Alsace kirsch to help with the digestion.

ALSACE WHITE WINE
1 VEAL TROTTER
1 CARROT
1 ONION
CLOVES
SALT
PEPPER
JUNIPER BERRIES
CUMIN
3.25 LB RAW
   SAUERKRAUT
1 LB SMOKED BACON
1 SAUCISSON
SAUSAGES, SMOKED
   BELLY OF PORK,
   HAM

Put in a big earthenware cocotte 1 quart of water plus 2 cups of Alsace wine, the veal trotter, one carrot, one onion studded with cloves, salt, pepper, juniper, a little cumin, and the sauerkraut—washed in fresh water and well squeezed. Leave to cook for an hour.

Add the smoked bacon and a *saucisson*—from Montbéliard, for example. Leave to cook again for an hour and, before the end of the cooking, add in all the Alsace specialties bought from the *charcutier*—sausages, smoked belly of pork, ham, etc.—all cooked.

Steam separately some potatoes to go with the choucroute.

Put on a warmer on the table and serve up bit by bit on hot plates.

♈ Alsace

COCHON DE LAIT FARCI ENTIER

WHOLE STUFFED SUCKLING PIG

1 MILK-FED
   SUCKLING PIG
SALT
PEPPER
SAUSAGE MEAT
FINES HERBES
OLIVES
SHALLOTS
MUSHROOMS
BUTTER

Salt and pepper the insides of the pig.

Fry the sausage meat before mixing with the chopped herbs, olives, shallots, and mushrooms, and then use it to line the insides of the pig. Sew up carefully, tying the feet under the body. Set the head straight with a skewer. Rub all over with butter, and put in the oven to roast or roast on a spit.

You have to allow at least 2 hours cooking, depending on the size. Baste often.

Present, and carve in front of the guests, accompanied with seasonable vegetables.

♇ Beaujolais nouveau

POTÉE AUVERGNATE

AUVERGNE PORK HOTPOT

1 PIG'S HEAD
2.25 LB LEAN BACON
1 HAM HOCK
CARROTS
TURNIPS
1 CELERIAC
ONIONS
BOUQUET GARNI
1 GREEN CABBAGE
WHITE HARICOT
   BEANS
POTATOES
1 BRAIN

Put the pig's head in a large marmite, along with the lean bacon and the ham hock. Cover with water and bring to a boil.

Skim and add the whole carrots, whole turnips, quartered celeriac, whole onions, and the bouquet garni. Cook for an hour.

Add the cabbage—blanched and quartered—and half-cooked beans. Cook on for another hour.

Add in the potatoes, quartered, and the brain. Cook for another 30 minutes and add in more boiling water if necessary.

To serve, drain the meats and carve into small pieces, except the brain. Lay the slices of meat on a large plate, surrounded by the vegetables.

♇ Beaujolais, red Hermitage

JAMBON FRAIS EN CROÛTE

HAM EN CROUTE

The ham should have been salted by syringe by your charcutier, *who has the brine and the saltpeter. Ask for a fresh ham large enough to feed all your guests. For the bread dough, you might use* Pâte à Brioche *(page 60).*

1 FRESH HAM
ONIONS
CARROTS
THYME
BAY LEAF
1 BOTTLE WHITE
  WINE
1 CUP PORT
BREAD DOUGH
1 EGG YOLK

Start in the oven, a first cooking of the ham with whole onions and quartered carrots, thyme, and bay. Moisten with white wine and port, and baste often.

Halfway through the cooking—allow 10 minutes per pound of ham—take the ham out of the oven, and let it cool enough to take off the rind, excess fat, and any bones.

Wrap the ham in bread dough, made ahead or bought in, and rolled to about ¾ inch thick. Paint with an egg yolk and cook on the bottom of the oven for another 10 minutes per pound.

Present and carve at the table.

Serve with spinach leaves or mushrooms in cream.

♀ Bordeaux, light red

(Opposite) Gaston Brazier, Eugénie's son

ANDOUILLETTE AU CHAMPAGNE

ANDOUILLETTE IN CHAMPAGNE

Andouillette is a smaller version of the coarse tripe sausage, andouille.

1 ANDOUILLETTE
PER PERSON
2 GLASSES
CHAMPAGNE
SALT
PEPPER

Warm the andouillette in a frying pan over a lively flame for 10 minutes or so.

Place in a gratin dish. Deglaze the frying pan with Champagne and pour over the andouillette. Salt, pepper, and place in the oven for 5 to 6 minutes.

Serve with a seasonal salad with bacon.

♆ Pouilly-Fumé, white Mâcon

COEUR DE VEAU BRAISÉ AUX CAROTTES

BRAISED VEAL HEART WITH CARROTS

Veal heart can also be cut into slices lengthwise and sautéed in butter, like a beefsteak.

1 VEAL HEART
PER PERSON
SMALL ONIONS
1 CUP BOUILLON
SALT
PEPPER
1 LB CARROTS
BUTTER

Warm the heart in a little butter and a few small onions.

When it is well colored, wet with bouillon or water. Season with salt and pepper. Add the carrots—cut into rounds if they are big winter carrots or left whole if they are new spring carrots. Cook on the stovetop for about an hour, covered.

Take out the heart and the carrots and keep warm. Degrease the cooking liquid and reduce right down to a small amount. Pour over the heart, cut into slices, accompanied by the carrots.

♆ Pinot noir, Beaujolais

FOIE DE VEAU À LA LYONNAISE

CALF'S LIVER LYONNAISE

*The liver of a calf that has grazed on herbs should have
a clear color.*

1 CALF'S LIVER
SALT
PEPPER
FLOUR
ONIONS
BUTTER
VINEGAR

Cut the liver into slices ½ inch thick. Season with salt and
pepper. Dredge in flour and fry in butter for about 4 minutes.

Place on a hot plate and cover with finely chopped onions,
sweated in butter.

Deglaze the frying pan with a little vinegar and pour over the
slices of liver.

♀ Beaujolais

FOIE DE VEAU AU VIN BLANC

CALF'S LIVER IN WHITE WINE

1 CALF'S LIVER
SALT
PEPPER
FLOUR
SHALLOTS
BUTTER
1 GLASS DRY WHITE
    WINE
PARSLEY

Cut the liver into slices ½ inch thick. Salt, pepper, and dredge
in flour.

In a cast-iron pan, sweat some finely chopped shallots in a good
piece of butter. As soon as they whiten, remove from the pan and
keep ready.

Put in their place the slices of liver and let them cook gently,
turning.

When beads of blood appear on the surface of the liver, put
the shallots back in the pan, as well as a good glass of dry
white wine. Stir well. Sprinkle with chopped parsley and serve
straightaway.

The liver can be served with a puree of potatoes.

♀ Beaujolais nouveau, light Côtes-du-Rhône

PIEDS DE VEAU GRILLÉS

GRILLED CALF'S TROTTERS

Calf's trotters should be sold already blanched. You can blanch them some more in boiling water for a few minutes. Refresh in cold water and finish the cleaning by taking off any extra hairs.

1 CALF'S TROTTER
  PER PERSON
BUTTER
ONIONS
CARROTS
SALT
PEPPER
MUSTARD
BREAD CRUMBS
SAUCE DIABLE
  (OPPOSITE)

Braise in butter with chopped onions and carrots for 30 minutes.

Salt and pepper. Split them in two, take out the bone, and coat with mustard. Baste in melted butter and roll in bread crumbs. Put them in the top of the oven to broil gently. Serve the *sauce diable* to the side.

♀ Beaujolais, red Côtes-du-Rhône

FRICASSÉE DE L'ARDÈCHE

ARDÈCHE FRICASSÉE OF KIDNEYS, LIVER, AND LIGHTS

POTATOES
1 OR 2 ONIONS
PORK FAT
PORK KIDNEYS
PORK LIVER
PORK LIGHTS
SALT
PEPPER
THYME
BAY LEAF
BLOOD SAUSAGE

Cut the potatoes into rounds, quite thick. Dice the onions and sauté everything in pork fat in a pan. Cook for about 10 minutes over a low flame.

When the potatoes are about half cooked, add the kidneys, a few slices of liver, and the lights, chopped up into pieces. Salt, pepper, and season with thyme and a bay leaf. Leave to cook gently for 30 minutes.

At the last minute, fry or broil the blood sausage and add to the fricasée. Serve straightaway.

♀ Red Côtes-du-Rhône

LANGUE DE VEAU À LA DIABLE

DEVILED CALF'S TONGUE

1 CALF'S TONGUE
SMALL ONIONS
2 OR 3 CARROTS
SALT
PEPPER
STOCK
MUSTARD
EGG
OIL
BREAD CRUMBS
SAUCE DIABLE
   (BELOW)

Leave the tongue in cold water for half a day or overnight, to clean before the preparation.

Blanch the tongue in salted boiling water for a few minutes. Take off the coarse skin and all the fat.

Braise in a cocotte with a few small onions, 2 or 3 carrots, salt, pepper, and a little stock or water. Leave to cook, covered, for 30 minutes. Reduce the cooking liquid. The tongue can be served straightaway as it is.

To devil the tongue, split down its length and coat with mustard. Dredge *à l'anglaise*—a mix of beaten egg, water, oil—and roll in bread crumbs. Broil lightly at the top of the oven and serve with the *sauce diable*.

Tongue is served with garden vegetables, puree of potatoes, or fresh noodles . . .

♉ Beaujolais, red Côtes-du-Rhône

SAUCE DIABLE

DEVIL'S SAUCE

1 ¼ CUPS WHITE
   WINE
3 OR 4 SHALLOTS
SAUCE TOMATE
   (PAGE 264)
SALT
PEPPER
CAYENNE PEPPER
FINE HERBES OR
   CHOPPED PARSLEY
   (OPTIONAL)

In a thick-bottomed pan, put the white wine and finely chopped shallots. Add a little *sauce tomate*. Season with salt, pepper, and a little cayenne. You can add chopped herbs or parsley depending . . .

PIEDS DE VEAU SAUCE POULETTE

VEAL TROTTERS WITH SAUCE POULETTE

1 CALF'S TROTTER
   PER PERSON
COURT BOUILLON
CARROTS
ONIONS
BOUQUET GARNI
SALT
PEPPER
BEURRE MANIÉ
   (PAGE 254)
HEAVY CREAM
2 EGG YOLKS
LEMON JUICE
PARSLEY

Blanch and clean the trotters as for *Pieds de Veau Grillés* (page 204). Braise the trotters for 35 minutes in an intense court bouillon with carrots, onions, bouquet garni, salt, and pepper.

Once cooked, slip off the bone and cut the meat into big pieces.

To make the *sauce poulette*, bind the cooking liquor with the *beurre manié*. Add a few spoons of heavy cream and, off the flame, 2 egg yolks—whipping vigorously—then a piece of fresh butter. Adjust the seasoning and add, according to your taste, some lemon juice.

Put the trotter pieces in the hot *sauce poulette* and sprinkle with chopped parsley.

Serve with rice or steamed potatoes.

♀ Beaujolais, red Côtes-du-Rhône

ROGNONS D'AGNEAU EN BROCHETTES

SHEEP'S KIDNEY KEBABS

4 SHEEP'S KIDNEYS
BACK BACON
MUSHROOMS
BUTTER
SALT
PEPPER
BEURRE MAÎTRE
   D'HÔTEL (PAGE
   254)

Open each kidney in two and take off the thin skin that covers them. Skewer them lengthwise, alternating with a piece of bacon and a mushroom head. Baste with melted butter. Salt, pepper, and broil under a high flame, but keeping the kidneys lightly pink.

Serve with the *beurre maître d'hôtel* to the side.

Accompany with Provençal tomatoes and matchstick potatoes.

♀ Beaujolais nouveau

ROGNON DE VEAU
À LA BERRICHONNE

BERRY-STYLE VEAL KIDNEY

1 VEAL KIDNEY
BUTTER
A PIECE OF HAM
MUSHROOMS
1 GLASS RED WINE
PARSLEY
SAUCE TOMATE
   (PAGE 264)
SALT
PEPPER
PARSLEY

The kidneys from young animals are always more tender than those from older ones.

Take the fat off the kidney, trim, and cut up into dice—not too small or they will toughen. In a frying pan, warm through in butter the ham, chopped up into big dice. Add in chopped raw mushrooms.

Remove the ham and mushrooms and, in the same butter, fry the pieces of kidney for a few minutes, being careful to keep them lightly pink. Drain and keep warm.

Deglaze the frying pan with a good glass of red wine. Add a little *sauce tomate*. Salt, pepper, and bring to a boil for a few instants.

Put back in the sauce the kidneys, ham, and mushrooms. Mix everything together well without letting it boil.

Serve straightaway garnished with chopped parsley.

Serve as is, without vegetables.

♉ Red Sancerre

ROGNON DE VEAU À LA CRÈME

VEAL KIDNEY IN CREAM

Buy kidneys that are firm and shiny.

1 VEAL KIDNEY
BUTTER
1 GLASS DRY WHITE
  WINE
SALT
PEPPER
HEAVY CREAM
1 EGG YOLK

Clean the kidney, taking off all the fat, and trim any nerve ends. Cut into slices that are not too thin. Sauté in hot butter in a frying pan.

Pour off the excess butter and deglaze with a good glass of dry white wine. Salt, pepper, and leave to reduce. Depending on the size of the kidney, whip a few spoons of heavy cream with an egg yolk and add in. Leave to warm through for a few moments.

Put the kidney slices back in the sauce. Stir, without letting it boil, and serve very hot.

♈ White Mâcon, Pouilly-Fumé

ROGNON DE VEAU FLAMBÉ
AU NOILLY-PRAT

VEAL KIDNEY FLAMBÉED IN VERMOUTH

4 SMALL VEAL
  KIDNEYS
FLOUR
BUTTER
SALT
PEPPER
3 GLASSES NOILLY-
  PRAT
STRONG MUSTARD

Trim the kidneys of any fat, finely dice, and flour lightly. Put ½ cup of butter in a pan. Warm the kidneys through over a high heat for 5 minutes; salt and pepper.

Deglaze the kidneys with Noilly-Prat. Flambé. Leave to reduce for 3 minutes. Incorporate a soupspoon of well-mixed, strong mustard.

At the moment of service—away from the heat—add a nut of butter. Mix the sauce well.

Serve with fresh noodles.

♈ White Mâcon, Pouilly-Fumé

ROGNON DE VEAU GRILLÉ

GRILLED VEAL KIDNEY

1 VEAL KIDNEY
SALT
PEPPER
BUTTER
BEURRE MAÎTRE
   D'HÔTEL
   (PAGE 254)

Trim the kidney, leaving a thin layer of fat all round. Cut in half lengthwise. Skewer on 2 sticks in such a butterfly fashion so that the halves of kidney will not close back on themselves during the cooking. Salt and pepper. Broil gently, basting the kidney often with melted butter.

Serve a *beurre maître d'hôtel* to the side.

℞ Beaujolais, red Côtes-du-Rhône

ROGNON DE VEAU AU MADÈRE

VEAL KIDNEY IN MADEIRA

1 VEAL KIDNEY
SALT
PEPPER
FLOUR
BUTTER
MADEIRA
MUSHROOMS
   (OPTIONAL)
PARSLEY

Trim the fat and any nerve ends from the kidney and chop into pieces—not too thin. Salt, pepper, and dredge lightly in flour. Fry in butter over a high heat, keeping the pieces lightly pink.

Remove and keep warm. Deglaze the frying pan with the Madeira or another sweet red wine. Check the seasoning and put the kidney back into the sauce. Stir the pan well to mix everything together without letting it boil.

You can, optionally, add into the sauce some mushrooms, sliced and sweated in butter.

Serve straightaway on very hot plates and sprinkle with finely chopped parsley.

℞ Rosé, red

TÊTE DE VEAU FARCIE

STUFFED CALF'S HEAD

1 DEBONED CALF'S
  HEAD
12 OZ PORK NECK
9 OZ VEAL
1 EGG
MUSHROOMS
SALT
PEPPER
SPICES (PEPPER,
  CLOVES, NUTMEG,
  CINNAMON)
ONIONS
CARROTS
BOUQUET GARNI
ROUX BLANC
  (PAGE 263)
COGNAC
TOMATO PUREE
HAM
BLACK OLIVES

At a triperie *you can usually find a deboned calf's head. Be sure it is fresh, because all offal can quickly smell bad.*

Take the calf's head, lay it out flat, and fill with a stuffing made of chopped pork neck, veal meat, a whole egg, chopped mushrooms, salt, pepper, and spices. The seasoning should be noticeable.

Roll up the head and sew up safely to hold the stuffing. Roll up in muslin; string both ends and the middle. Put on to cook in cold, salted water adding chopped onions, carrots, and the bouquet garni. Leave to cook very slowly for 5 hours.

Make a *roux blanc*. Add in a little of the cooking stock from the calf's head and a little Cognac. Add a spoon of tomato puree, some sliced ham, some pitted olives, and leave to cook for a few minutes.

Carve the head into thick slices and pour on the sauce.

Can be served with steamed or mashed potatoes.

♇ All red wines

TÊTE DE VEAU VINAIGRETTE

CALF'S HEAD VINAIGRETTE

½ CALF'S HEAD
1 SPOON FLOUR
SALT
PEPPER
½ GLASS VINEGAR
1 ONION
2 CARROTS
SAUCE VINAIGRETTE
   (PAGE 264)
1 SHALLOT
PARSLEY
1 EGG

Place the calf's head in a casserole of cold water. Let it boil for 15 minutes and refresh in cold water.

Cut into big pieces.

In a casserole, mix the flour in cold water. Put in the calf's head pieces with salt, pepper, half a glass of vinegar, the onion, and chopped carrots. Let it cook gently, covered with a tea towel but not a lid. Allow about 90 minutes. Do not overcook it and check with a fork.

Serve warm with a *sauce vinaigrette*, a chopped hard-boiled egg and chopped parsley.

Can be served with a few steamed potatoes.

♈ Rosé, light red

TABLIER DE SAPEUR

BREADED TRIPE

1 LB TRIPE
SALT
PEPPER
1 EGG YOLK
OIL
BREAD CRUMBS
BUTTER
SAUCE BÉARNAISE
   (PAGE 255)

Cut squares out of the tripe with sides of 3 inches. Boil them, refresh in cold water, and wipe them dry. Salt, pepper, and dip *à l'anglaise*—a mix of beaten egg yolk, water, and oil—and then dredge in the bread crumbs.

In a large pan, warm a good piece of butter and color the sides of tripe. You can slide the pan into the oven for a few moments to make it crisper.

Serve on hot plates. Accompany with steamed potatoes and a well-seasoned *sauce béarnaise*.

♈ White Mâcon

PIEDS-PAQUETS MARSEILLAIS

TRIPE AND TROTTERS MARSEILLE

LEAN BACON
PARSLEY
2 CLOVES GARLIC
SHEEP'S TRIPE
OIL
1 CARROT
1 ONION
1 LEEK
SHEEP'S TROTTER
DRY WHITE WINE
TOMATOES
SALT
PEPPER

Make a stuffing with the bacon, parsley, and a clove of garlic.

Cut the tripe into squares and make up into little parcels filled with the stuffing and fixed with a stick.

In an earthenware marmite, warm through in oil the chopped onion, carrot, and leek. Add a clove of garlic.

Blanch the trotter, put in the bottom of the marmite, and lay the tripe parcels on top. Cover with the white wine. Add a few quartered tomatoes. Salt and pepper, and seal hermetically. Bake in the oven for as long as possible, at least 90 minutes.

Before serving, degrease the cooking liquid. Arrange the trotters and the tripe parcels on a plate and sieve the sauce over them.

♀ Rosé de Provence

GRAS-DOUBLE À LA LYONNAISE

TRIPE LYONNAISE

1 LB COOKED TRIPE
3 LARGE ONIONS
PARSLEY

Boil cooked tripe—which you can get from the butcher—refresh in cold water, and dry it well with linen cloth. Dice the tripe into small batons.

Dice equally the onions, and fry everything in a large pan. Cover and leave to cook for about 15 minutes.

Sprinkle with chopped parsley. Serve straightaway, on hot plates.

♀ White Mâcon

TRIPES À LA MODE DE CAEN

TRIPE CAEN

In the old days, the cooking of tripe was entrusted to a local boulanger. That time has gone now. This recipe is only served in certain restaurants, where it is a specialty.

9 LB BEEF TRIPE
2 ONIONS STUCK
   WITH 4 CLOVES
   EACH
8 CARROTS
BOUQUET GARNI
6 LEEKS
2 VEAL TROTTERS
4 PORK RINDS (BELLY)
2½ TABLESPOONS
   SALT
2 TEASPOONS PEPPER
TOMATO PUREE
CIDER
1 GLASS CALVADOS
FLOUR

Buy the tripe raw. Leave to soak and clean in cold water for half a day or the night before preparing it.

Blanch in plenty of salted water for 15 minutes. Wash again in fresh water, drain. Divide the tripe into pieces of about 2 inches.

Preferably, you need a stone *triperie*, which has a small lid and can be hermetically sealed. If not, then a big saucepan with a lid. Put in the bottom all the vegetables and condiments, then the tripe, and in the middle the trotters and the pork rind.

Season with salt and pepper, put in the tomato puree. Cover the tripe with half cider and half water and add the Calvados. Close the marmite or triperie, after adding a flour-and-water paste. Start to cook over the flame and then in a gentle oven for 10 hours.

This dish needs to be served very hot, in very hot bowls.

♀ White Sancerre, Pouilly-Fumé

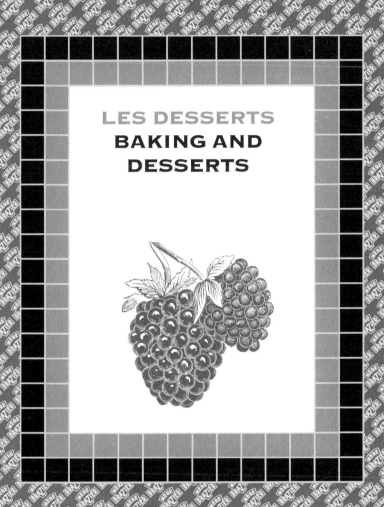

LES DESSERTS
BAKING AND
DESSERTS

BISCUIT AUX AMANDES

ALMOND BISCUIT

This biscuit can be cut into bands and garnished with chocolate. Almond biscuit can often be used instead of Pâte à Génoise *(opposite) and* Pâte à Biscuit de Savoie *(below).*

2⅓ CUPS
    CONFECTIONERS'
    SUGAR
3½ CUPS GROUND
    ALMONDS
12 EGGS, SEPARATED
¼ CUP ALL-PURPOSE
    FLOUR
¼ CUP BUTTER
OIL

Mix the confectioners' sugar and the ground almonds together, and then add in the egg yolks. Add the flour and melted butter. Whip up the egg whites into snow and fold them in carefully.

This biscuit is cooked on a flat oven sheet with a low rim. Cover it with aluminum foil and oil well. Spread out the biscuit mix to a maximum of ¾ inch. Bake in a medium oven—a few minutes should be enough.

PÂTE À BISCUITS DE SAVOIE

SAVOY BISCUITS

These biscuits can be eaten as they are or with jam, cream, or butter.

7 EGGS, SEPARATED
1⅓ CUPS SUPERFINE
    SUGAR
1 CUP ALL-PURPOSE
    FLOUR
PINCH OF SALT
⅔ CUP CORNSTARCH
VANILLA (OPTIONAL)
ALMONDS
    (OPTIONAL)
BUTTER

Work the egg yolks and the sugar to obtain a good white mix that folds into ribbons that wrap around each other.

Sift in the flour and the salt, then the cornstarch, and finally the vanilla.

Whisk the egg whites to very firm snowy peaks and fold into the pâte with a wooden spoon. Use straightaway.

Butter a round or square mold. You can scatter some crushed almonds around the dish.

Half-fill the mold with the biscuit mix. Bake in a moderate oven for 25 minutes. Cool on a rack, out of the oven.

PÂTE À BISCUITS À LA CUILLER

TEA BISCUITS

Small variations on this recipe have different names like ladyfingers, champagne biscuits. This can also form the base of an Omelette Norvégienne *(page 238).*

5 EGGS, SEPARATED
⅔ CUP SUPERFINE
  SUGAR
1¼ CUPS ALL-PURPOSE
  FLOUR
¼ CUP CORNSTARCH
BUTTER

Whisk the egg yolks with ½ cup of sugar until smooth. Add the flour and cornstarch and fold in the whites of the eggs, beaten to very firm peaks.

Pipe this mix onto a buttered and floured baking sheet to make little, thumb-sized chips. Dust well with a covering of superfine sugar. Shake off any excess sugar from the sheet and bake in a very gentle oven for about 5 minutes.

Keep in a metal tin until needed.

PÂTE À GÉNOISE

GENOISE BISCUITS

Génoise *can keep a few days before being used. They can be covered with cream, butter,* Crème Pâtissière *(page 233), or some jam.*

⅔ CUP SUPERFINE
  SUGAR
PINCH OF SALT
4 EGGS
1 CUP ALL-PURPOSE
  FLOUR
⅓ CUP CORNSTARCH
½ TEASPOON YEAST
BUTTER (OPTIONAL)

Whisk slowly the sugar, the salt, and the eggs over a low flame to get a smooth, consistent pâte.

Take off the heat and keep whisking until cold. Add the flour, cornstarch, and yeast carefully, stirring to be sure not to have any lumps.

Grease and flour a mold, pour in the mixture, and bake in a hot oven for 20 minutes.

You can add to the *pâte à génoise* ¼ cup of melted butter, but it is not essential.

SOUFFLÉ CHAUD

HOT SOUFFLÉ

The trick is to whisk the egg whites at the last minute and to serve the soufflé straight from the oven. The guests can wait . . . a soufflé won't.

2 CUPS MILK
SALT
¼ CUP SUPERFINE
   SUGAR (PLUS EXTRA
   FOR THE MOLD)
¼ CUP BUTTER
   (PLUS EXTRA FOR
   THE MOLD)
½ CUP ALL-PURPOSE
   FLOUR
5 EGGS, SEPARATED
FLAVORING
   (AS YOU LIKE)

Bring the milk to a boil, with a pinch of salt and a little sugar.

In a thick-bottomed pan, melt the butter, add in the flour, and cook lightly without letting it color. Add in the boiling milk and keep stirring with a wooden spoon.

Take off the heat at the first boil, but keep stirring. Off the heat, add the egg yolks, one by one, and keep working. Add the chosen flavor here, if you like.

Whisk to build the egg whites into a firm snow. Fold carefully into the soufflé mix just before it is ready to go in the oven.

Butter and sugar a soufflé mold. Fill halfway up with the soufflé mixture and put in a medium oven—too hot and the soufflé will catch and turn out badly. Allow 35 minutes to bake.

SOUFFLÉ AU CHOCOLAT: Add 1 cup of melted chocolate to the milk before incorporating the eggs.

SOUFFLÉ À LA LIQUEUR: Flavor the soufflé mixture with a small glass of alcohol (Grand Marnier, Kirsch, Green Chartreuse, as you choose) before adding the egg whites.

SOUFFLÉ AUX FRAISES DES BOIS OU AUX FRAMBOISES

WILD STRAWBERRY OR RASPBERRY SOUFFLÉ

WILD STRAWBERRIES
    OR RASPBERRIES
KIRSCH
SOUFFLÉ CHAUD
    (OPPOSITE)
STRAWBERRY OR
    RASPBERRY EAU
    DE VIE

Macerate the fruits for an hour or two in the kirsch.

In the soufflé dish, make a layer of fruit, then a layer of soufflé mix, then more fruit . . .

Flavor the soufflé mixture with the eau de vie.

BANANES SOUFFLÉES

BANANA SOUFFLÉ

BANANAS
SOUFFLÉ CHAUD
    (OPPOSITE)
RUM
BUTTER
SUPERFINE SUGAR

Cut open the bananas lengthwise, convex side up, and take out the flesh. Put in a mixer with the soufflé mix and a splash of rum. Then add the egg whites and fill the banana skins with the mixture.

Set up in a buttered gratin dish. Bake for about 8 minutes in a hot, but not too hot, oven. Take them out of the oven and sprinkle with sugar, baste with rum, and flambé at the table.

SOUFFLÉ GLACÉ
AU GRAND MARNIER

COLD GRAND MARNIER SOUFFLÉ

1 CUP SUPERFINE
  SUGAR
8 EGG YOLKS
1 GLASS GRAND
  MARNIER
1 CUP HEAVY CREAM
COCOA POWDER

Make a syrup with one cup of water and the sugar. Bring to a boil and leave to cool.

Whisk this syrup into the 8 egg yolks over heat, just to the point of boiling. Keep working as they cool down. Add a glass of Grand Marnier.

Whisk up a *crème Chantilly*, and fold into the egg yolks carefully.

Line the inside of the soufflé mold with aluminum foil to raise the edges. Pour in the soufflé mix and leave in the refrigerator overnight.

When the soufflé has set, tear off the aluminum foil. The soufflé should have risen around one inch above the rim of the mold.

Sprinkle over some cocoa powder. Decorate with additional *crème Chantilly*.

BAVAROIS

BAVARIAN CREAM

Bavarois can be scented with alcohol or with a puree of fruit, like ice cream. They used to make beautiful copper molds for bavarois, *but they are difficult to find now.*

8 EGGS
1 CUP SUPERFINE
  SUGAR
2 CUPS MILK
7 LEAVES GELATIN
ALCOHOL/PUREED
  FRUIT
2 CUPS HEAVY CREAM

Work the egg yolks with the sugar to a smooth paste. Pour over the boiling milk and leave to cook for a few minutes without letting it boil again.

Leave to cool, stirring often. Before the mix has completely chilled, soak the gelatin leaves in cold water and add the alcohol or fruit puree.

Whip up a very firm *crème Chantilly*. Fold gently into the mix.

Pour into a mold and put in the refrigerator for a few hours.

Serve with *crème Chantilly*.

PÂTE À QUATRE-QUARTS

FRENCH POUND CAKE

This cake will keep in a tin for a few days. You can equally decorate them with cream, butter, or jam.

4 EGGS
1 CUP SUPERFINE
  SUGAR
2 CUPS ALL-PURPOSE
  FLOUR
1 TEASPOON SALT
1 TEASPOON YEAST
1 GLASS MILK
1 CUP BUTTER

Whisk the eggs and the sugar for 10 minutes.

Add the flour, salt, yeast, and milk. Work for a few minutes, then incorporate the creamed butter. Pour into a mold and bake in a hot oven for 25 minutes.

CHARLOTTE

CHARLOTTE

1 VANILLA POD
1 CUP MILK
1 CUP WILD
  STRAWBERRIES
⅓ CUP RASPBERRIES
KIRSCH
SUPERFINE SUGAR
4 EGG YOLKS
4 LEAVES GELATIN
1 CUP HEAVY CREAM
9 OZ PÂTE À BISCUITS
  À LA CUILLER
  (PAGE 219)

Careful! Don't use any kirsch if this cake is destined for children.

Infuse a vanilla pod, split in two lengthwise, in boiling milk.

Macerate the strawberries and raspberries in the kirsch.

Work the sugar and egg yolks together until smooth, then pour on the hot milk—without the vanilla—whisking strongly all the time. Leave to cool. Dissolve the gelatin in cold water and add to the mix.

Whisk the cream into a *crème Chantilly* with sugar, and fold in to the egg-yolk mixture. Add any kirsch leftover from macerating the fruits. Add the fruit into the mix.

Line the bottom of a charlotte mold with a sheet of aluminum foil to make it easier to lift out later.

Carpet the bottom and sides with crushed biscuits that have been splashed with kirsch.

Fill the mold with the egg and milk mix. Cover with a plate and leave overnight in the refrigerator.

Turn out on to a plate and garnish with additional *crème Chantilly*.

CLAFOUTIS

CLAFOUTIS

Clafoutis can work as a number of variations—pear, plum, apple, prune.

2 ½ CUPS ALL-
PURPOSE FLOUR
1½ TEASPOONS
YEAST
3 EGG YOLKS
1⅔ CUPS
GRANULATED
SUGAR
PINCH OF SALT
RUM OR KIRSCH
BUTTER
CHERRIES

Sift the flour and yeast.

Work the egg yolks and sugar to create a smooth white paste. Carefully fold in the flour and yeast, salt, and your chosen flavoring—kirsch or eau de vie, for example.

Butter and sugar a sheet of aluminum foil and line a flan dish with it. Arrange in it some very ripe cherries, pitted and stalks off. Pour over the egg and flour mixture and bake in a medium oven for 45 minutes.

PÂTE À MADELEINES

MADELEINES

You can flavor these madeleines with the zest of lemon or a splash of rum.

17 WHOLE EGGS
2 ½ CUPS SUPERFINE
SUGAR
1 TABLESPOON
BAKING SODA
5 CUPS ALL-PURPOSE
FLOUR
½ CUP BUTTER,
MELTED
LEMON ZEST
(OPTIONAL)
RUM (OPTIONAL)
BUTTER AND FLOUR
FOR THE PAN

Whisk together the eggs and sugar, add the baking soda and the flour. Work for a few minutes and add the melted butter. Leave the pâte to rest for an hour before using.

Butter and flour lightly a madeleine pan and fill with the mix. Bake in a hot oven for about 10 minutes, depending on size.

CONFITURE DE CERISES OU DE FRAISES

CHERRY OR STRAWBERRY JAM

La Mère used the Baumé scale—marked as "B"—developed by French pharmacist Antoine Baumé in 1768 to measure the density of various liquids as either heavier or lighter than water, with distilled water at 0.

CHERRIES OR
STRAWBERRIES
PRESERVING SUGAR

Weigh the fruit. Weigh up half as much sugar. Melt the sugar in a little water. Reduce to get a syrup at 37°B—2 pounds of sugar to 1 quart of water, boiled and left to cool.

Throw the fruit into this syrup and leave to cook for 10 minutes without boiling.

Drain the fruit. Put the syrup back on the fire and reduce again to bring the syrup's density back to 37°B.

Put the fruit back in and cook for another 10 minutes to bring the density back to 37°B and cook again, for 20 minutes, without letting it boil. Leave to cool before potting.

CONFITURE D'ORANGES

ORANGE JAM

ORANGES
PRESERVING SUGAR

Pick oranges that are medium sized, thin-skinned, and untreated. Prick all over with a fork and leave to soak in fresh water for 3 days, changing the water twice a day.

Boil up in plenty of water until you can pierce the oranges with a straw.

Refresh for a few hours and then cut them into rounds.

Weigh and add an equal amount of sugar. Cook for about an hour, skimming often.

CONFITURE DE COINGS

QUINCE PRESERVE

The quince, even when very perfumed, is never eaten raw. From quinces you can get a jelly, jam, pâte, etc . . .

QUINCES
PRESERVING SUGAR

JELLY: Peel some very ripe quinces. Take out the seeds and wrap them in muslin. Cut up the quinces. Put them straight into water, with some lemon so they do not turn yellow. Put the quince into a marmite, cover with water, add the seeds in the muslin cloth. The quince is cooked when it can be easily squashed in your fingers. Sieve the juice and put back on the fire with an equal amount of sugar. Add a few squeezes of lemon and orange. The jelly is cooked when a skin forms easily on a cold plate.

JAM: Prepare as above. When the quinces are cooked, sieve—still hot—through a cloth. Add half as much sugar in weight and bring to a boil, stirring all the time with a spatula, for at least 45 minutes.

PÂTE: Add an equal amount of sugar to the sieved quince and cook for 90 minutes to 2 hours, stirring regularly. Spread out on aluminum foil about ¾ inch thick, and leave to dry in a warm space for 2 weeks. Cut up into big rectangles and keep in a metal tin.

CONFITURE DE PRUNES OU D'ABRICOTS

PLUM OR APRICOT JAM

PLUMS OR APRICOTS
PRESERVING SUGAR

Separate the fruits. Take out the pits. Leave to macerate in three-quarters of their weight in sugar for 24 hours. Cook for an hour, stirring gently with a wooden spoon.

OMELETTE FLAMBÉE À LA CONFITURE

OMELET FLAMBÉ

You can replace the jam with wild strawberries, raspberries steeped in kirsch, or raspberry eau de vie.

5 EGGS
½ CUP SUPERFINE
　SUGAR
RUM OR KIRSCH
¼ CUP BUTTER
5 SPOONS
　CONFITURE
　D'ABRICOT
　(PAGE 229)
CONFECTIONERS'
　SUGAR

Warm an oval, ovenproof plate in the oven.

Break and whisk the eggs, add the sugar, and the rum or kirsch. Make the omelet in a pan just like an unsweetened omelet (page 46).

When cooked, lay on the warm plate. Fill the middle with the apricot jam, or other filling, fold over and turn down the edges.

Sprinkle with confectioners' sugar. Warm a metal skewer over a flame and when it is red hot, draw a pattern on the omelet. Baste with a glass of kirsch or rum, depending on the filling, and flambé in front of the guests.

PÊCHES OU ABRICOTS AU SIROP

PRESERVED PEACHES OR APRICOTS

PEACHES OR
　APRICOTS
SUPERFINE SUGAR

Choose fruit that is not too ripe. Choose yellow-fleshed peaches. Take off the peach skin by dunking the fruit in boiling water for a few seconds. Split in two and take out the pit. Pile them up in jars.

Fill up with a syrup made of 4 cups sugar to 4 cups of water, brought to a boil and then cooled. Put the jars in a marmite filled with warm water. Bring to a boil for 15 minutes and leave to cool in the marmite.

Conserved fruits like this can be eaten as a compote or used to garnish a tart.

CRÈME ANGLAISE

CUSTARD SAUCE

1 VANILLA POD
I QUART MILK
8 EGG YOLKS
1 CUP SUPERFINE
SUGAR

Split the vanilla pod in half and add to the milk. Bring to a boil and allow the vanilla to infuse.

Work the egg yolks and the sugar together, until smooth and white.

Take the vanilla pod out of the milk and pour over the egg-and-sugar mix, whisking vigorously.

Work for a few minutes over a flame without letting it boil. Sieve into a stainless-steel bowl. Give it a few more whisks as it cools.

ÎLE FLOTTANTE

FLOATING ISLAND

8 EGG WHITES
1½ CUPS
CONFECTIONERS'
SUGAR
⅔ CUP ALMONDS
CARAMEL (SEE
RECIPE)
½ CUP CRÈME
ANGLAISE
(ABOVE)

Whisk the egg whites into a firm snow. Sweeten with confectioners' sugar, and mix in the almonds, crushed.

Line a Pyrex mold with caramel. Pour in the mixture and bake in a bain-marie in a medium oven for about 30 minutes.

Unmold, while still warm, onto a plate that is spread with *crème anglaise*. Serve very fresh.

CARAMEL: La Mère used caramel to garnish and flavor her molds for baking. Warm an aluminum pan and add sugar. Leave it to melt—about 5 minutes—when the edges turn liquid. Shake a few times. Go slowly. Then use a wooden spoon to stir as the crystals turn to liquid. About 10 minutes. Take off the heat and add a spoon or two of water—which will make it all splutter—stir out any lumps.

OEUFS À LA NEIGE

SNOW EGGS

5 EGG WHITES
⅓ CUP CONFECTIONERS' SUGAR
1 QUART MILK
CRÈME ANGLAISE (PAGE 231)

Whisk the egg whites into a very firm snow and, at the last minute, sweeten with the confectioners' sugar.

Warm the milk in a big enough pan. As soon as it trembles, poach the egg whites taking it one spoonful at a time. Let the whites cook for 2 to 3 minutes, turning them. Lift out carefully and drain on a towel.

Use the milk to make a *crème anglaise* with plenty of vanilla.

Make a little caramel (page 231) and pour over each egg.

Let the *crème anglaise* cool. Serve very cold with the eggs on top.

CRÈME RENVERSÉE OU FLAN

BAKED CUSTARD

1⅓ CUPS SUPERFINE SUGAR
5 EGGS
5 EGG YOLKS
1 QUART MILK

Work the sugar, eggs, and egg yolks until smooth and white.

Bring the milk to a boil and pour into the mix, whisking all the time.

Pour into a Pyrex mold and bake in a bain-marie in a medium oven for an hour.

CARAMEL: Line a Pyrex dish with caramel (page 231), making sure the sides are well coated. Pour in the egg and sugar mix and cook in the mold as above.

COFFEE: Add to the milk a few spoons of coffee.

CHOCOLATE: Melt chocolate in the milk.

CRÈME PÂTISSIÈRE

PASTRY CREAM

4 EGG YOLKS
1 CUP SUPERFINE
　SUGAR
1 CUP ALL-PURPOSE
　FLOUR
1 QUART MILK

Work the egg yolks with the sugar. Add in the flour.

Bring the milk to a boil and pour onto the egg and sugar mix. Put it back over a flame and keep whisking until it boils. Pour into a bowl and keep mixing while it cools. Do not store it in an aluminum receptacle.

PÂTE À BABA (SAVARIN)

RUM BABA

1¼ CUPS ALL-PURPOSE
　FLOUR
½ TEASPOON SALT
1½ TEASPOONS
　SUGAR
2 EGGS
1 TEASPOON YEAST
SCANT ½ CUP MILK
¼ CUP BUTTER
RUM OR KIRSCH
CRÈME PÂTISSIÈRE
　(ABOVE)
PRESERVED FRUIT
CRÈME CHANTILLY
CORINTHIAN RAISINS
　(OPTIONAL)

With this recipe you can make little babas. You can also add some Corinthian raisins into the mix, macerated in rum.

Sift the flour into a bowl, add the salt, sugar, eggs, and the yeast dissolved in warm milk. Whisk hard and add the melted butter. Keep working for a few minutes. The pâte should be quite sloppy. Add more milk if necessary.

Grease a mold and pour in the mix. Leave to rise in a warm environment, uncovered. Bake in a medium oven for about 20 minutes.

Taking it out of the oven, wet with a syrup at 20°B—4 cups of sugar diluted in 4 cups of water, brought to a boil and allowed to cool—and kirsch or rum. Make sure the cake is well soaked.

Fill the middle with a *crème pâtissière* flavored with a little kirsch and some chopped preserved fruits. Garnish with *crème Chantilly.*

Serve cold.

PÂTE À CRÊPES, PÂTE À GAUFRES

SWEET CRÊPE AND WAFFLE BATTER

2 CUPS ALL-PURPOSE
FLOUR
2 TABLESPOONS
SUGAR
4 EGGS
PINCH OF SALT
2 CUPS COLD MILK
¼ CUP BUTTER

In a large bowl, whisk the flour, sugar, eggs, and salt. When the mix is supple, add the milk. The batter needs to be fairly liquid, but it will thicken as it rests. Leave to stand for 2 hours.

When you are about to use it, color the butter in a pan until it is nutty. Whisk into the batter.

GALETTE DES ROIS À LA PAYSANNE

KINGS' CAKE

½ CUP
CONFECTIONERS'
SUGAR
¾ CUP GROUND
ALMONDS
2 EGGS
¼ CUP BUTTER
¼ CUP ALL-PURPOSE
FLOUR
CRÈME PÂTISSIÈRE
(PAGE 233)
PÂTE FEUILLETÉE
(PAGE 58)
1 EGG YOLK

Traditionally this is eaten in France on Twelfth Night. Don't forget to hide a king and a queen inside!

Mix the confectioners' sugar with the ground almonds, and then add in the 2 eggs. Add in the melted butter and the flour. Mix into this an equal amount of *crème pâtissière*. This is a frangipane.

Roll out a sheet of *pâte feuilletée* into a circle about ¼ inch thick. Garnish with the frangipane, leaving a border of ¾ inch. Wet the border with a little water and cover with another sheet of *pâte feuilletée* of equal size. Carefully seal the edges with the back of a knife. Wash the package with an egg yolk. Decorate with a few cuts using the point of a knife. Bake in a hot oven for 30 to 40 minutes.

Serve warm.

CRÊPES ODETTE

ODETTE'S CRÊPES

Reinette apples keep admirably well.

REINETTE APPLES
BUTTER
PÂTE À CRÊPES
(OPPOSITE)
GRANULATED SUGAR
RASPBERRY EAU
DE VIE

Peel and core the apples and cut into very thin (1/10 inch) rounds. Fry them gently in butter without letting them break up.

In a large, buttered pan, add a thin layer of crêpe batter, then a layer of apple, then a new layer of batter. Cook on both sides, turning over carefully.

Turn out onto a large plate. Sprinkle over some sugar, splash with raspberry eau de vie, and flambé.

Serve very hot.

CRÊPES SUZETTE

CRÊPES SUZETTE

This recipe is usually prepared in front of the guests.

PÂTE À CRÊPES
(OPPOSITE)
1 ORANGE
6 TO 7 SUGAR CUBES
1 GLASS COGNAC
1 GLASS GRAND
MARNIER
BUTTER
SUPERFINE SUGAR

Prepare 3 very thin crêpes for each person. Rub the sugar cubes over the skin of the orange to extract the oils.

Warm a long metal plate, and add in the Cognac, Grand Marnier, and a nut of butter.

Warm through and put the sugar cubes in, to melt in the mix. Be careful not to let the mix burn, because it can easily burst into flames in contact with the heat.

When everything has dissolved, soak the pancakes in the alcohols and let them drink up the juices, turning with a fork. Fold the pancakes into four on the plate. Sprinkle with superfine sugar and flambé with a little more Grand Marnier.

CRÊPES SOUFFLÉES

SOUFFLÉ CRÊPES

PÂTE À CRÊPES (234)
CRÈME PÂTISSIÈRE
(PAGE 233)
EGG WHITES
BUTTER
KIRSCH

Cook the crêpes and fill with *crème pâtissière* mixed with egg whites, whisked to a firm snow.

Roll up the crêpes, place in a buttered dish, split in half, and put in a hot oven for 15 minutes.

Baste with kirsch and flambé.

RIZ À L'IMPÉRATRICE EUGÉNIE

RICE PUDDING EMPRESS EUGENIE

PRESERVED FRUIT
GOLDEN RAISINS
ALCOHOL (YOUR
CHOICE)
1 HANDFUL RICE PER
PERSON
MILK
SUGAR
VANILLA
CRÈME ANGLAISE
(PAGE 231)
GELATIN
CRÈME CHANTILLY

The night before, macerate the preserved fruits, chopped into big cubes, and the raisins in the alcohol—rum, Cognac, maraschino (cherry liqueur), as you choose.

Cook the rice in water for 5 or 6 minutes. Drain. Finish the cooking in sugared milk with vanilla. Allow about 20 minutes. The rice should be well cooked. Rinse under clean water and leave to cool.

Make a *crème anglaise*, into which you dissolve a few leaves of gelatin.

Mix the macerated fruit with the rice and incorporate the *crème anglaise* and a little *crème Chantilly*. Place in a round mold and leave in the refrigerator for 24 hours.

Turn out and decorate with *crème Chantilly*.

LA MÈRE'S
CLASSIC MENU No.6

Fonds d'Artichauts Périgourdine
Artichokes with Truffle (page 56)

◆

Quenelles au Gratin
Quenelles Gratin

◆

Volaille Demi-Deuil
Chicken in Half-mourning (page 142)

◆

Fromages
Cheeses

◆

Glace Vanille ou Chocolat Chaud
Vanilla Ice Cream (page 238)
or Hot Chocolate

GLACES

ICE CREAM

Be careful preparing ice cream—it can easily sour, causing serious problems. Always eat freshly made ice cream, because freezing overnight does it no favors. If that is the case then melt, put back in the sorbetière *(ice cream maker), and start again.*

8 EGG YOLKS
1½ CUPS SUPERFINE
    SUGAR
1 QUART MILK
FLAVORING
1 CUP HEAVY CREAM

Work the egg yolks with the sugar until they turn white.

Add to boiling milk, whisking all the time. Cook for a few minutes and keep working as it cools down.

Add the flavors . . . all kinds of alcohols, caramel, coffee, vanilla, almonds, etc.

Build the ice cream up in a *sorbetière* and add heavy cream at the last moment.

OMELETTE NORVÉGIENNE

NORWEGIAN OMELET (BAKED ALASKA)

PÂTE À BISCUITS À LA
    CUILLER (PAGE 219)
ICE CREAM (ABOVE)
EGG WHITES
CONFECTIONERS'
    SUGAR
RUM OR KIRSCH

Lay up on a silver or a stainless-steel plate some crushed *biscuits à la cuiller*. Onto this base, spoon out some ice cream—vanilla, coffee, nut, or another flavor—to about 2 inches high. Cover again with another layer of crushed biscuits.

Whisk the egg whites to snow, enough to cover the whole omelet. Sweeten with confectioners' sugar. Using a piping bag, cover the sides and top of the ice cream with the egg whites.

Put the tray on a second tray of crushed ice and place under a red-hot broiler. Let it color lightly.

At the table, baste with rum or kirsch and flambé. The omelet should have plenty of volume to impress the guests.

PUDDING FAÇON MÈRE BRAZIER

MÈRE BRAZIER'S PUDDING

To use up stale petits fours and leftovers, la Mère would make this pudding for the staff. It is so delicious it could have been served to the guests.

ICE CREAM
  (OPPOSITE)
1 LB PETIT FOURS
CARAMEL (PAGE 231)

To the ice cream mixture, add broken-up stale petits fours, perhaps left over from a reception.

Make a caramel in a charlotte mold, and line the bottom and sides.

Pour the ice cream and petits four mix into the mold and bake in a bain-marie for about 45 minutes.

Leave to cool. Put in the refrigerator overnight and serve the next day.

SORBETS

SORBET

Sorbets are ice creams based on purees of fruits with a sugar syrup. You get the juice by sieving crushed fruit through a fine linen cloth. Remove any seeds or the results will be bitter. These ices, very digestible, are good value when the fruit is in season. They can accompany a crème Chantilly. *To serve, they can go back into the empty skin of the fruit—oranges, lemons, pineapples, for example.*

FRUIT PUREE
SUPERFINE SUGAR
ALCOHOL

Mix the juice from the pulp with the syrup at 30°B—4 cups of sugar for 1 cup of boiled water.

Mix to obtain a liquid weighing 18°B on a syrup scale. Improve the flavor of the fruit by adding an equivalent alcohol. Put in a *sorbetière*.

PARFAIT GLACÉ

ICED PARFAIT

Flavor this recipe with coffee, chocolate, vanilla, alcohol, or a puree of fruit.

1 PINT HEAVY CREAM
4 EGG YOLKS
1 CUP SUGAR
FLAVOR (AS YOU LIKE)

Whisk up the cream as for a *crème Chantilly*—the cream needs to be quite liquid, and kept cold in the refrigerator.

Work the egg yolks with the sugar until you get a white, smooth paste. Carefully fold in the Chantilly. Add the flavoring.

Pour into a mold and refrigerate for 4 or 5 hours.

Serve garnished with *crème Chantilly*.

MOUSSE AUX FRAISES OU AUX FRAMBOISES

STRAWBERRY OR RASPBERRY MOUSSE

This is what we call an Italian meringue mix.

1 ⅓ CUPS FRUITS
1 CUP SUPERFINE
   SUGAR
5 EGG WHITES
CRÈME CHANTILLY

Blend the fruit in a mixer.

Cook the sugar to 257°F to achieve a blond caramel—what we call cracked.

Whisk the egg whites into a firm snow and fold in, carefully, the cracked sugar. Keep whisking until completely cold and then add in the fruits.

Pour into tall glasses and leave in the refrigerator for a few hours.

Serve with a *crème Chantilly*.

MOUSSE AU CHOCOLAT

CHOCOLATE MOUSSE

*You can add peeled almonds—roasted and chopped—
or chopped Orange Jam (page 228).*

9 OZ CHOCOLATE
BUTTER
5 EGGS (SEPARATED)
RUM

Melt over a very gentle heat the chocolate with a little water and
a nut of butter. Away from the fire, incorporate, one at a time, the
egg yolks, stirring with a wooden spoon. Add the rum.

Whisk the egg whites into a firm snow. Fold them delicately
into the chocolate and put them into tall glasses. Refrigerate
overnight.

PÂTE BRISÉE

SHORT PASTRY

This recipe serves as a base for fruit tarts, flans . . .

FOR ONE TART OF 8
    PORTIONS:
5 CUPS ALL-PURPOSE
    FLOUR
2 TEASPOONS SALT
3 EGGS
1 CUP BUTTER

Sift the flour on to a marbled surface or a table. Make a well in
the middle. Add salt, eggs, and melted butter.

Work with your fingertips to ensure a homogenous mix. Bash it
3 times, which is to say smash the dough under the palm of your
hand. Gather it up into a ball, wrap in linen, and leave out until
the next day.

TARTE AUX FRUITS

FRUIT TART

PÂTE BRISÉE
(PAGE 241)
HEAVY CREAM OR
CRÈME PATISSIÈRE
(PAGE 233)
FRUIT

FOR APPLES AND PEARS: Make a *pâte brisée* base in a circular tart dish ⅕ inch thick. Prick the base with a fork. Cover with a layer of heavy cream. Circle the dish with thin slices of apple or pear without overlapping. Sprinkle with superfine sugar and bake in a hot oven for 30 to 35 minutes. Serve still warm.

FOR PEACHES, APRICOTS, AND PLUMS: Poach the fruits in a vanilla syrup for a few minutes. Leave to drain.

Line the tart dish with a layer of *pâte brisée* ¼ inch thick. Prick the bottom with a fork and cook in the oven for 10 minutes. Fill the tart base with a layer of *crème pâtsissière* (page 233), flavored with a little kirsch. Arrange the drained fruits on the cream and drizzle over some sieved apricot juice from a jam or conserve.

FOR RASPBERRIES AND STRAWBERRIES: Follow the same recipe as above except use raw fruit and drizzle over some warm gooseberry jelly to which you can add a little gelatin to help it set.

GOOSEBERRY GELÉE

GOOSEBERRY JELLY

La Mère often used gooseberry jelly as a glaze.

4 LB GOOSEBERRIES
1 LB SUGAR

Simmer 4 pounds of gooseberries in 2 quarts of water until collapsed. Sieve overnight.

Bring the juice to a boil with 1 pound of sugar to 2 cups of liquid.

Check for setting on the back of a cold plate.

TARTE AU CITRON, À LA MANDARINE, OU À L'ORANGE

LEMON, MANDARIN, OR ORANGE TART

PÂTE BRISÉE
(PAGE 241)
¼ CUP BUTTER
¾ CUP SUPERFINE
SUGAR
3 TABLESPOONS ALL-
PURPOSE FLOUR
2 TABLESPOONS
CORNSTARCH
2 EGGS, SEPARATED
1 LEMON
SCANT ½ CUP
CONFECTIONERS'
SUGAR

Take a circular tart tin and make a base of *pâte brisée*, being careful to make sure the sides are at least ¾ inch high. Allow 10 minutes baking.

Bring 1 cup of water to a boil with the butter and the sugar. Add in the flour and the cornstarch and stir with a wooden spoon for a few minutes over the fire.

Off the heat, add in 2 egg yolks, the juice of the lemon, and its finely grated zest. Leave this cream to cool and then fill the tart dish with it.

Whip the egg whites into a firm snow, sweeten with confectioners' sugar and cover the tart.

Bake in a very hot oven for a few minutes to lightly color.

MILLAS

MILLAS

EGG YOLKS
½ CUP SUPERFINE
SUGAR
½ CUP BUTTER
1 CUP ALL-PURPOSE
FLOUR
PINCH OF SALT
2 EGGS
RUM OR KIRSCH
1 PINT MILK
9 OZ PÂTE BRISÉE
(PAGE 241)
CHERRIES

This can be made with cherries or very ripe Bartlett pears.

In a bowl, work the egg yolks and the sugar to achieve a good white paste. Add the melted butter, the flour, the salt, the whole eggs, then the rum or kirsch. Add the milk slowly, stirring all the time.

Line a flan dish or circular tart dish with a thin layer of *pâte brisée*.

Choose very ripe cherries, take off the stalks, and pit them. Cover the *pâte brisée* with 2 layers. Fill up with the millas mix. Bake in a hot oven for about 30 minutes.

TARTE TATIN

TART TATIN

The original recipe used a copper mold, but today's silicone works well enough, even if it lacks a little thickness.

½ CUP PLUS
   2 TABLESPOONS
   BUTTER
2½ CUPS SUPERFINE
   SUGAR
2 LB REINETTE APPLES
SWEETENED PÂTE
   BRISÉE (PAGE 241)

You need a flameproof round mold with a rim of at least 1½ inches. Line the bottom of the mold with butter, cut into slices. Cover with the sugar.

Core and cut the apples into large quarters and fill the mold up to a height of 1⅓ inches.

Cover the apples with a layer of *pâte brisée*, one-fifth of an inch thick, making sure to stick the pastry dough well to the inside of the mold. Bake in a hot oven for 25 minutes.

Put the mold on a high flame for 3 minutes, shaking to get the caramel out of the apples. Turn out on to a plate and serve straight away, because the caramelization from the apples, sugar, and butter will not work so well when cold.

PÂTE À BUGNES DE LYON

LYON-STYLE ANGEL WINGS

4 CUPS ALL-PURPOSE
   FLOUR
¼ CUP SUGAR
1 TEASPOON SALT
4 EGGS
1½ TEASPOONS
   YEAST
¼ CUP BUTTER
ORANGE WATER
CONFECTIONERS'
   SUGAR

Make the dough the night before.

Sift the flour and make a well. Add the sugar, salt, eggs, yeast, melted butter, and orange water. Knead to a firm paste. Keep working and pulling out to give it as much body as possible. Roll up into a ball, wrap in linen, and leave out overnight.

Split into 2 balls and roll out as thin as possible. Cut out rectangles of between 2 and 3 inches. Roll out the rectangles so they are as thin as a piece of paper. Deep-fry, turning. Sprinkle with confectioners' sugar.

BEIGNETS

FRITTERS

2 ½ CUPS ALL-
    PURPOSE FLOUR
2 EGGS
1 TABLESPOON
    SUGAR
1 TEASPOON SALT
¼ CUP BUTTER
⅔ CUP BEER
FLAVORING

Sift the flour into a bowl. Add the eggs, sugar, salt, melted butter, the beer, and scant cup of warm water. Work for a few minutes and then leave to rest for an hour.

BANANA FRITTERS : Cut a banana into rounds. Spike the pieces on a fork, dip into the batter, and throw into the fryer. Leave to go golden, then take out and drain. Arrange on a plate and sprinkle with sugar and serve very hot.

APPLE FRITTERS : Peel and core the apples—Reinette, for choice. Cut into thin slices. Plunge into the batter, deep-fry, and serve sprinkled with sugar. Serve very hot.

ACACIA FLOWER FRITTERS : Be careful, not all acacia are edible. Soak a bunch of whole flowers in the batter, agitate a little so they are well covered. Deep-fry and serve them on a plate with absorbent paper. Dust with sugar.

PÂTE À FRIRE

FRYING BATTER

If you are making a dessert or sweet dish, the batter can be flavored with rum, kirsch, or Cognac.

2 CUPS ALL-PURPOSE
    FLOUR
4 EGGS
1 TEASPOON SALT
1 GLASS BEER
1 GLASS MILK
OIL (OPTIONAL)

Work the flour with 2 egg yolks, 2 whole eggs, and the salt. Add the beer and the milk. Keep the batter liquid; if not, when frying it may not stick to the pieces imprisoned within.

You can add a tablespoon of oil to the mix and, equally, at the time of use, 2 whipped egg whites.

PÂTE À CHOUX

SWEETENED CHOUX PASTRY

1 TABLESPOON SALT
2 TABLESPOONS
    SUGAR
1 CUP BUTTER
3 CUPS ALL-PURPOSE
    FLOUR
12 EGGS

In a thick-bottomed casserole, warm 2 cups of water with the salt and sugar. Add the butter, and then, as it comes to a boil, add the sifted flour in one go. Stir hard with a wooden spoon until the dough is well homogenized and leaves the sides of the pan.

Leave it to cool a little and incorporate, one at a time, the whole eggs, stirring all the time. Leave the dough for an hour to rest.

PETS-DE-NONNE

RUM CHOUX

The tricky bit is that these fritters have to be prepared at the very last minute.

SWEETENED PÂTE
    CHOUX PASTRY
    (ABOVE)
RUM
CONFECTIONERS'
    SUGAR
OIL FOR FRYING

Make a sweetened *pâte à choux* and flavor it with a splash of rum.

With a little spoon, lift out little balls and put them on to deep-fry. Let them color for about 3 minutes.

Lift out and drain on absorbent paper. Sprinkle with confectioners' sugar and serve very hot.

PÂTE À MERINGUE ORDINAIRE

MERINGUE

Flavor these meringues with coffee extract or cocoa powder.

8 EGG WHITES
SCANT 4 CUPS
   CONFECTIONERS'
   SUGAR
OIL

Whisk the egg whites into very firm peaks. Sift over the confectioners' sugar so it rains. Keep whisking for 10 minutes.

Lay up immediately on an oiled sheet pan and put in the oven at 120°F to dry out, not to cook.

POMMES BONNE FEMME

BAKED APPLES

1 REINETTE APPLE PER
   PERSON
SUGAR
BUTTER
GOOSEBERRY JELLY

Wipe clean equal-sized Reinette apples. Core them and cut slits into the sides all the way round and about halfway up. Butter a gratin dish and put the apples in. Put ¾ inch of water into the gratin dish or, better still, the juice from a jar of preserved fruits.

Fill the holes in the apple with sugar and put a knob of butter on each apple. Bake in a hot oven for 30 minutes.

Take them out of the oven and garnish with gooseberry jelly.

Serve warm in the cooking dish.

GALETTE BRESSANE

BRESSE GALETTE

*At La Mère, this brioche-style cake was invariably offered with
vanilla ice cream and covered with hot chocolate.*

5 CUPS ALL-PURPOSE
FLOUR
6 EGGS
SALT
1½ CUPS SUPERFINE
SUGAR
1 CUP MILK
2 TEASPOONS YEAST
2 CUPS GOOD BUTTER

The night before: Sift the flour into a bowl and make a well in the
center. Break the eggs into the middle. Add a pinch of salt, the
sugar, the cup of milk—warmed, and in which the yeast has been
allowed to melt. Knead well, so the pâte takes some shape. Add
the creamed butter and keep kneading for a quarter of an hour.
Leave to rise in the warm for an hour. Rework the dough, cover
with a linen cloth, and put in the refrigerator.

On the day: Work the dough again and roll out to a thickness of
about 1 ½ inches. Lay up in a deep, round mold. Leave to rise in
the warm for 1 or 2 hours, where there is some air flowing.

When the dough has risen well, cover across its surface, 15
or so nuts of butter and then cover well with additional
superfine sugar.

Put in a hot oven for 30 minutes.

☙ Brut Champagne

PÊCHES GLACÉES FLAMBÉES AU KIRSCH

PEACHES FLAMBÉED WITH KIRSCH

These were always served with Galette Bressane *(opposite),*
still warm from the oven. You can use canned peaches or fresh
peaches cooked in syrup.

2 TO 3 PEACH HALVES PER PERSON PEACH SYRUP BUTTER ALMONDS 1 GLASS KIRSCH	Drain the peaches and keep the syrup. Generously butter a large ovenproof dish. Lay in the peach halves and put in about ¾ inch deep of syrup. Sprinkle generously over the peaches some peeled, chopped almonds. Put in the oven for about 30 minutes. Take out of the oven and serve straightaway, pouring over the peaches a warmed glass of kirsch. Flambé in front of your guests. Serve with a spoon of ice cream to the side of the fruit. ♈ Brut Champagne

CHABRANINOF

CHABRANINOF

This was the cult dessert in our restaurant in rue Royale—it owes
its name to the four people who all helped create it—Jo Chatelus,
Gaston Brazier, Michel Nivert, and Georges Ivanof.

4 GOLDEN DELICIOUS APPLES BUTTER SUPERFINE SUGAR 1 GLASS RUM 2 CUPS VANILLA GLACES (PAGE 238) PÂTE À GAUFRES (PAGE 234)	Peel and core 4 Golden Delicious apples. Cut them into eighths. Warm through in butter until they color. Put them in an ovenproof dish, sprinkle with superfine sugar, and place in a very hot oven. Leave to caramelize. Take out of the oven and flambé with a small glass of rum at the table. Serve with vanilla ice cream and waffles.

LES BEURRES ET LES SAUCES
BUTTERS AND SAUCES

BEURRE D'AIL

GARLIC BUTTER

7 OZ GARLIC CLOVES
1¼ CUPS BUTTER

Blanch the garlic cloves. Put them in a blender with the butter. Blend and push through a sieve, if necessary.

BEURRE D'AMANDES

ALMOND BUTTER

3.5 OZ SKINNED
ALMONDS
1 CUP BUTTER

In a blender, put a spoon of cold water, the almonds, and butter. Blend and pass through a sieve, if necessary. Use the same quantities and methods for pistachio and other nut butters.

BEURRE D'ANCHOIS

ANCHOVY BUTTER

3.5 OZ ANCHOVIES
1¼ CUPS BUTTER

Wash, clean, and drain the anchovies. Put into the blender with the butter. Blend and push through a sieve, if necessary.

BEURRE BERCY

BERCY BUTTER

SCANT CUP WHITE
WINE
1 SHALLOT
2 CUPS BUTTER
1 LB BONE MARROW
SALT
PEPPER
1 LEMON

Reduce by half the white wine with the finely chopped shallot. Let the reduction cool and add the butter and the poached and drained bone marrow, chopped into little pieces. Add salt, a grind of pepper, and the juice of the lemon.

BEURRE D'ÉCREVISSES

SHRIMP BUTTER

This butter can have many uses.

SHRIMP SHELLS
1 CUP BUTTER
4 CUPS WATER

Crush the shrimp shells. Add the butter and leave the mix to cook slowly. The butter will become red. Leave it to clarify and add the water. Boil up for a few minutes.

Leave to cool. If it is not cold enough, put in the refrigerator to chill. The butter will have solidified on the surface. Take it off.

Melt the butter again and sieve through a linen cloth. Leave to cool and keep in the refrigerator.

BEURRE D'ESCARGOTS

SNAIL BUTTER

Every fantasy is allowed to personalize this recipe—nuts, anchovy butter, bacon . . .

2 CUPS BUTTER
PARSLEY
3 SHALLOTS
GARLIC
SALT
PEPPER
LEMON JUICE

It is a question of carefully mixing the butter with the finely chopped parsley and the shallots very, very finely chopped. It is traditional, also, to use some garlic, but you can take it out at the end. Season with salt and pepper and a little lemon juice.

You can also add in roasted chopped nuts, a little *Beurre d'Anchois* (opposite) or a little bacon fat, cut up very finely.

BEURRE MAÎTRE D'HÔTEL

MAÎTRE D'HÔTEL BUTTER

1¼ CUPS BUTTER
PARSLEY
SALT
PEPPER
1 LEMON
MUSTARD (OPTIONAL)

Soften the butter. Incorporate into it a good spoon of chopped parsley, salt, a grind of pepper, and the juice of the lemon.
You can add a good spoon of mustard. Roll this butter into a cylinder, wrap in baking paper or aluminum foil, and place in the refrigerator. Cut into rounds and place on broiled fish fillets.

BEURRE MANIÉ

BEURRE MANIÉ

½ CUP BUTTER
¾ CUP FLOUR

Melt the butter. Incoporate into it the flour. Leave to cool a few minutes. This *beurre manié* is the binder for many sauces. Careful: a sauce thickened with a *beurre manié* should not be allowed to boil, as it risks taking on the flavor of the cooked flour.

AILLOLI

AIOLI

GARLIC
SALT
EGG YOLKS
OLIVE OIL
LEMON

You can make this sauce in the traditional way with a pestle and mortar, or in a mixer. For every 4 cloves of garlic, allow 1 egg yolk and 1 cup of olive oil. In the mortar, put the garlic, salt, and the egg yolk and build up as for a *sauce mayonnaise* (page 259), pouring the oil in 1 drop at a time. If using a mixer, you can put the garlic, egg, salt, and oil all in together in one go. When the sauce has thickened, add the lemon juice and a few drops of hot water to cut the fat. *Ailloli* accompanies steamed or broiled fish, and all kinds of vegetables.

SAUCE BÂTARDE

BASTARD SAUCE

½ CUP FLOUR
1¾ CUPS BUTTER
5 EGG YOLKS
2 TABLESPOONS
   HEAVY CREAM
1 LEMON

Mix the flour with 3 tablespoons melted butter. Wet with 3⅓ cups of boiling, salted water. Whisk vigorously and bring to a boil. Leave to cool, then bind with the egg yolks mixed with the cream and the juice of the lemon. Bring back to a boil. Sieve through a linen cloth and finish off with the remaining butter, away from the heat. Once done, keep the sauce ready in a bain-marie until you are ready. This sauce can be served with asparagus or poached fish.

SAUCE BÉARNAISE

BÉARNAISE SAUCE

½ GLASS WINE
   VINEGAR
1 SHALLOT
TARRAGON
CHERVIL
A PINCH OF SALT
PEPPERCORNS
6 EGG YOLKS
2½ CUPS BUTTER
PARSLEY
PEPPER (OPTIONAL)
PAPRIKA (OPTIONAL)
LEMON (OPTIONAL)

In a small, thick-bottomed casserole, warm the wine vinegar with a finely chopped shallot, chopped tarragon, bruised chervil, the salt, and a few crushed peppercorns. Leave to reduce almost completely.

Take off the fire, leave to cool. Add the egg yolks mixed with a little water. Whisk these eggs over a low flame or in a bain-marie. Keep whisking all the time, so as not to get scrambled eggs.

When the eggs have taken a good consistency, add, a little at a time, hot melted butter. Be careful not to pour on the milk at the bottom of the pan. The sauce should take on the same consistency as a mayonnaise. Check the seasoning and add in at the end, a good spoon each of chopped tarragon and parsley. And if you want, depending on its use, you can add pepper, paprika, or lemon juice.

Keep warm in a *bain-marie*.

♀ Always a grand white wine from Burgundy or Alsace

SAUCE BÉCHAMEL

BÉCHAMEL SAUCE

This sauce is the base for many recipes in this book.

MILK
BEURRE MANIÉ
   (PAGE 254)
5 OZ VEAL
1 ONION
PEPPER
SALT
NUTMEG
BOUQUET GARNI
BUTTER

Bring enough milk to a boil for your recipe. Bind with a *beurre manié*, whisking up to the first boil. Dice the veal. Chop the onion and sweat in butter. Add the veal and onion to the milk. Season with pepper, salt, and a little finely grated nutmeg—careful, not too much. Add the bouquet garni and leave to cook for an hour. Sieve the sauce and keep warm in a bain-marie. To stop the surface wrinkling while it is waiting, pour a little melted butter on top to cover.

SAUCE CHANTILLY

CHANTILLY SAUCE

SAUCE MAYONNAISE
(PAGE 259)
CRÈME CHANTILLY

Chantilly sauce is simply a mayonnaise to which you add some *crème Chantilly* to lighten it (without vanilla). Serve with asparagus.

SAUCE DUXELLES

MUSHROOM SAUCE

ONIONS
BUTTER
SHALLOTS
MUSHROOMS
SALT
PEPPER

Peel and chop the onions, and sweat in butter. Add diced shallots and chopped, pressed mushrooms. Season with salt and pepper. Leave to cook until it is completely dry. We use this sauce for our gratins.

Or put scant 1 cup white wine in a thick-bottomed casserole pan, with scant 1 cup of the cooking liquor from the mushrooms and 3 finely chopped shallots. Let it reduce by half. Then add 2 tablespoons of tomato puree and 4 tablespoons of *sauce duxelles* mix, as above. Check the seasoning. Leave to boil. Add ½ soupspoon of chopped parsley.

SAUCE AUX FINES HERBES

HERB SAUCE

1 SHALLOT
PARSLEY
CHERVIL
WHITE WINE
CHICKEN VELOUTÉ
(PAGE 266) OR
SAUCE BÉCHAMEL
(PAGE 255)
4 SPOONS HEAVY
CREAM
TARRAGON

Put the diced shallot, the parsley stalks, and bruised chervil into the white wine and reduce by half. Add 2 cups of chicken velouté or not-overly-thick béchamel. Bring to a boil for a few minutes and then sieve. Add the heavy cream and a teaspoon of chopped tarragon. Season with salt and pepper. This sauce can go with poached eggs, with chicken, with sweetbreads.

SAUCE GRIBICHE

GRIBICHE SAUCE

6 EGGS
1 TEASPOON MUSTARD
SALT
PEPPER
2 CUPS OLIVE OIL
1 SOUPSPOON
 VINEGAR
GHERKINS
CAPERS
PARSLEY
CHERVIL
TARRAGON

Hard-boil the eggs. In a large bowl, crush the yolks. Add the mustard, salt, and pepper. Work until smooth. Build the sauce up, whisking in the olive oil drop by drop as for a *sauce mayonnaise* (page 259). Add the vinegar. Finish it by adding diced gherkins and capers. Add a large spoon each of chopped parsley, chervil, and tarragon. Garnish with the slices of 3 egg whites. This sauce accompanies cold meats and fish.

SAUCE HOLLANDAISE

HOLLANDAISE SAUCE

You can add to a sauce hollandaise *one-third of its volume of very firm and unsweetened* crème Chantilly *(whipped cream).*

6 EGG YOLKS
2½ CUPS BUTTER
LEMON
SALT (OPTIONAL)

Pour a glass of salted water into a small casserole pan with a thick bottom. Add the egg yolks. Cook over a very low flame or in a bain-marie, whisking all the time.

When the yolks have taken on a good consistency, add, little by little, hot, melted butter, being careful not to pour into the little layer of milk that will have formed at the bottom of the pan. Keep whisking until all the butter has been incorporated and the sauce has the consistency of mayonnaise.

Add lemon juice and salt if needed. Do not use any pepper—the little gray specks look bad.

This sauce is also served with chicken, sweetbreads, and asparagus.

SAUCE HONGROISE

HUNGARIAN SAUCE

1 ONION
6 TABLESPOONS
  BUTTER (PLUS EXTRA
  FOR SWEATING)
1 TEASPOON PAPRIKA
1 GLASS DRY WHITE
  WINE
BOUQUET GARNI
1¼ CUPS VELOUTÉ
  (PAGE 266)
3 SPOONS HEAVY
  CREAM

Sweat the chopped onion in butter without letting it color. Season with the paprika. Wet with the dry white wine. Add in the bouquet garni. Leave it to reduce by two-thirds. Add the *velouté*. Leave to cook slowly for 20 minutes, adding in toward the end the heavy cream. Sieve and finish at the last moment with the 6 tablespoons of butter. This sauce goes with veal, chicken, and poached fish.

SAUCE LYONNAISE

LYONNAISE SAUCE

ONIONS
BUTTER
SCANT CUP VINEGAR
SCANT CUP WHITE
  WINE
SCANT 2 CUPS
  SAUCE TOMATE
  (PAGE 264)

In a thick-bottomed pan, sweat some roughly chopped onions in butter. Let them whiten very slowly. The onions should be almost cooked. Add the vinegar and white wine. Reduce by two-thirds. Add the *sauce tomate*. Cook very slowly for 5 to 6 minutes. Sieve. Depending on your taste and the nature of the dish, you can leave the onions in and not sieve it.

SAUCE MAYONNAISE

MAYONNAISE

Be sure that both the oil and the eggs are at room temperature. Dribble the oil in very slowly at the start. If the sauce turns, it can be saved by starting again with a fresh egg yolk. But you can quickly succeed with a mayonnaise by adding all the ingredients in a blender.

SALT
VINEGAR
4 EGG YOLKS
2 LARGE SPOONS OF
   MUSTARD
WHITE PEPPER
2 PINTS OIL
LEMON

Dissolve the salt in a little vinegar. Add the egg yolks, the mustard, and white pepper. Build the sauce up with a whisk, pouring in the oil very slowly. Finish with a squeeze of lemon.

Finally add a few spoons of boiling water, which makes it less oily and stops it from turning.

To sauce a fish, add a few leaves of gelatin dissolved in boiling water. You can also add into the mayonnaise a little tomato puree.

SAUCE MOUTARDE À LA CRÈME

MUSTARD CREAM SAUCE

3 SOUPSPOONS
   MUSTARD
SALT
PEPPER
1 LEMON
HEAVY CREAM

In a bowl, mix the mustard with salt, pepper, and the juice of a lemon. Build up the sauce as if making a *Sauce Mayonnaise* (above) but instead of olive oil use a thick, fresh, heavy cream. A good sauce for hors d'oeuvres.

SAUCE NANTUA

NANTUA SAUCE

SAUCE BÉCHAMEL
   (PAGE 255)
HEAVY CREAM
BEURRE D'ÉCREVISSES
   (PAGE 253)
SHRIMP TAILS

Mix scant 1 cup of heavy cream to 4 cups of béchamel. Reduce by one-third and bring it back to its normal consistency by adding more cream.

To finish, add 5 ounces *beurre d'écrevisses* and 20 or so shrimp tails. Serve with fish gratins or quenelles.

SAUCE NEWBURG

NEWBURG SAUCE

1 (1.75-LB) LOBSTER
5 TABLESPOONS
    BUTTER
4 TABLESPOONS
    OLIVE OIL
SALT
CAYENNE PEPPER
1 GLASS COGNAC
1 GLASS MADEIRA
SCANT CUP HEAVY
    CREAM
SCANT CUP FISH
    FUMET

Cut up the live lobster. Lift off the creamy parts and the roe, crush with 2 tablespoons of butter, and keep them back.

Cook the tail, claws, and head of the lobster with 3 tablespoons of butter and 4 tablespoons of olive oil. Season with salt and cayenne pepper.

When the shells are bright red, drain off the fat. Wet with warmed Cognac and flambé. Add the Madeira. Reduce by two-thirds.

Add the cream and fish fumet. Leave to cook slowly for 25 minutes.

Take out all the lobster flesh and chop into dice. Sieve the sauce and add in the roe butter. Check the seasoning and mix in the lobster dice before serving.

This sauce is served with a fish like a salmon, a trout, a sole . . .

SAUCE NORMANDE

NORMANDY SAUCE

3 CUPS FISH VELOUTÉ
SCANT ½ CUP
    MUSHROOM
    COOKING LIQUOR
SCANT ½ CUP MUSSEL
    COOKING LIQUOR
SCANT CUP SOLE
    FUMET
5 EGG YOLKS
1¼ CUPS THICK
    HEAVY CREAM
½ CUP PLUS
    2 TABLESPOONS
    BUTTER
SALT
PEPPER

Add the fish velouté to the mushroom and mussel cooking liquors. Add, as well, a sole fumet made with the sole bones and a few squeezes of lemon. Bind with egg yolks mixed with the heavy cream. Reduce over a high flame by a good third.

Sieve the sauce and finish it with the remaining heavy cream and the butter. Check the seasoning of salt and pepper.

For garnish, use the mushrooms and mussels used in the cooking.

This sauce is especially good accompanying sole, but can also be used for other fish such as turbot and salmon.

SAUCE PÉRIGUEUX

TRUFFLE SAUCE

VELOUTÉ (PAGE 266)
VEAL GELATIN
1 GLASS WHITE
    BORDEAUX
1 TEASPOON
    COGNAC
BUTTER
TRUFFLES

Make the *velouté* with a brown roux (page 263). Place in a bain-marie and add in a little veal gelatin, the wine, and the Cognac. Leave to reduce for 15 minutes. Thicken the sauce with butter and add, for 2 cups of sauce, about 5 ounces of diced truffle. Leave to simmer for 10 minutes.

SAUCE PIQUANTE

PIQUANT SAUCE

1¼ CUPS WHITE WINE
1¼ CUPS WINE
    VINEGAR
3 TO 4 SHALLOTS
2½ CUPS SAUCE
    TOMATE (PAGE 264)
3 GHERKINS
CHERVIL
PARSLEY
TARRAGON

In a thick-bottomed casserole, pour in the white wine, the wine vinegar, finely chopped shallots, and the *sauce tomate*. Cook for 10 minutes. After the cooking, and off the fire, add chopped gherkins, chervil, parsley, and tarragon.

This sauce is usually served with broiled or roasted pork. We also serve it with boiled beef.

SAUCE PORTUGAISE

PORTUGUESE SAUCE

1 LARGE ONION
OLIVE OIL
1.5 LB TOMATOES
1 CLOVE GARLIC
SALT
PEPPER
SUGAR (OPTIONAL)
SAUCE TOMATE
    (PAGE 264)
PARSLEY

Dice the onion finely and warm in olive oil. As the onion whitens, add the tomatoes—skinned, seeded, and quartered—the garlic, salt, pepper, and a little sugar if the tomatoes are too acidic. Cover and let cook slowly. Taste to evaluate and add some *sauce tomate* if it is not strong enough. Add, at the last minute, a soupspoon of chopped parsley.

SAUCE POULETTE

POULETTE SAUCE

1 SHALLOT
¼ CUP BUTTER
SCANT ½ CUP DRY
   WHITE WINE
SCANT CUP HEAVY
   CREAM
2 EGG YOLKS
SALT
PEPPER
PARSLEY

Chop the shallot and sweat in butter. Wet with the dry white wine and leave to reduce by half. Add the cream, bring to a boil, then take off the fire. Bind the sauce with 2 egg yolks. Salt, pepper, and sprinkle over some chopped parsley.

SAUCE RÉMOULADE

RÉMOULADE

4½ CUPS SAUCE
   MAYONNAISE
   (PAGE 259)
3.5 OZ GHERKINS
2 OZ CAPERS
PARSLEY
CHERVIL
TARRAGON
ANCHOVY PUREE

To the mayonnaise, add chopped gherkins, chopped capers, a soupspoon each of chopped parsley, chervil, and tarragon, and a soupspoon of anchovy puree. To accompany celeriac, sheep's trotters.

SAUCE RAVIGOTE

RAVIGOTE SAUCE

VINEGAR
1 SHALLOT
BAY LEAF
CHERVIL
TARRAGON
THYME
SCANT ½ CUP FISH
   FUMET
SCANT 1 CUP SAUCE
   BÉCHAMEL
   (PAGE 255)
6 TABLESPOONS
   BUTTER

Mix the finely chopped shallot with the bay, a few sprigs of chervil, chopped tarragon, and thyme in the vinegar. Reduce by two-thirds. Then add the fish fumet and béchamel. Leave to cook a few moments, whisking all the time. Finish with the butter and sieve. At the last moment, add a spoon of chervil and a spoon of chopped tarragon. This sauce can accompany broiled fish.

ROUX

ROUX

Be careful cooking butter. It can easily blacken and would give a disagreeable flavor to any sauce made with it.

½ CUP BUTTER
1 ½ CUPS FLOUR

WHITE ROUX: Warm the butter without letting it color. Add the flour. Mix well with a wooden spoon. Cook over a soft flame, stirring all the while, for 5 minutes. This roux is used to prepare a white sauce or a *velouté* (page 265).

BLOND ROUX: The same recipe as for a white roux but, in the cooking, let the mix take a light blond color. This roux is used for many sauces for poultry, sweetbreads . . .

BROWN ROUX: The same recipe as for the blond roux, but cook longer to brown the flour. You can use margarine, which has less of a tendency to burn.

SAUCE SUPRÊME

SUPREME SAUCE

CHICKEN
VEAL
VEAL HOCK
HEAVY CREAM
BUTTER

When poaching a chicken, add a piece of veal and a veal hock. Keep the cooking liquid and leave it to reduce for a long time. When the *velouté* has reached a good consistency, add a few tablespoons of heavy cream. Check the seasoning. At the moment of service, add a good piece of butter.

SAUCE TARTARE

TARTAR SAUCE

8 EGGS
SALT
PEPPER
2 PINTS OLIVE OIL
1 SOUPSPOON
  VINEGAR
CHIVES

Hard-boil the eggs. Mash the yolks, or put in a mixer to get a smooth paste. Salt, pepper, and build up as for a mayonnaise with olive oil. Finish with the vinegar and chopped chives.

This sauce also goes with fish, cold meats, or chicken.

SAUCE TOMATE

TOMATO SAUCE

According to la Mère, if you don't have fresh tomatoes, you can use tomato puree.

3 TO 4 SHALLOTS
BUTTER
6.5 LB TOMATOES
1 SPRIG THYME
1 BUNCH PARSLEY
2 CLOVES GARLIC
1 BAY LEAF
SALT
PEPPER

Thinly slice the shallots and sweat in butter in a big marmite. Add the tomatoes—chopped in quarters—the thyme, parsley, garlic, bay, salt, and pepper. Cover the marmite and leave to cook slowly for 30 to 35 minutes. Pick out the cloves of garlic without crushing them. Sieve the sauce and cover the surface to stop any skin forming. Put in a terrine and, when the sauce is cold, keep in the refrigerator. But be careful: This recipe will not keep very long in the refrigerator. You have to freeze it to keep longer.

SAUCE VINAIGRETTE

LA MÈRE'S VINAIGRETTE

1 SOUPSPOON FINELY
  CHOPPED ONION
1 SOUPSPOON
  CHOPPED PARSLEY
1 SOUPSPOON
  CHOPPED CHERVIL
1 SOUPSPOON
  CHOPPED
  TARRAGON
1 SOUPSPOON
  CHOPPED CAPERS
SALT
PEPPER
SCANT ½ CUP RED
  WINE VINEGAR
1¼ CUPS OLIVE OIL

In a bowl put, in order, the onion, parsley, chervil, tarragon, capers, salt, a grind of pepper, the red wine vinegar, and the olive oil. Mix well.

Sometimes you can add chopped hard-boiled eggs.

LA MÈRE'S CLASSIC MENU NO.7

Served every year on November 11

Boudin et Godiveaux Grillés
Grilled Sausages

Pommes-Frites Sautées
Sautéed Potatoes

Rôti de Porc
Roast Pork

Marrons et Épinards à la Crème
Chestnuts and Spinach in Cream

Pâté à Baba
Rum Baba (page 233)

Glace à Vanille
Vanilla Ice Cream (page 238)

Galette

VELOUTÉ

VELOUTÉ

The name of this recipe translates literally as "velvety." A proper velouté, as defined by Carême, would be thickened with a roux of flour and butter, but la Mère would often bind hers with a cholesterol-rich blend of cream and eggs refined with truffle, as in her Velouté de Volaille (page 143).

WHITE ROUX
(PAGE 263)
STOCK
BUTTER

Make the white roux. Add chicken, veal, or fish stock. This stock should be well reduced and warm to achieve a smooth *velouté*. Bring to a boil, stirring. After the boil, turn down the fire and cook slowly for an hour. Sieve and pour into a terrine. Pour on a skin of warm butter to stop it from wrinkling.

SAUCE VERTE

GREEN SAUCE

Watercress can be very fragile, but it will keep for more than a couple of days if kept in some frequently changed cold water.

2 OZ WATERCRESS
2 OZ SPINACH
2 OZ PARSLEY
2 OZ CHERVIL
3¾ CUPS SAUCE
MAYONNAISE
(PAGE 259)

In a casserole of boiling salt water, throw in the watercress, spinach, parsley, and chervil. Cook for 5 minutes. Drain and dry. Chop the leaves and squeeze in a towel to get the juice. You should have a scant ½ cup. Mix this juice with a thick mayonnaise. To go with cold fish or cold white meats.

GELÉE

ASPIC JELLY

This was how we used to make a meat gelée.

9 LB HOCK AND VEAL
    BONES
3.25 LB OTHER
    BROKEN VEAL
    BONES
3 BLANCHED VEAL
    TROTTERS
9 OZ BLANCHED PORK
    RIND (BELLY)
7 OZ CARROTS
7 OZ LARGE ONIONS
2 OZ LEEKS
2 OZ CELERY
BOUQUET GARNI
SALT
PEPPERCORNS
1 LB LEAN BEEF
6 EGG WHITES
MADEIRA, COGNAC,
    ALSACE WINE, OR
    CHAMPAGNE

Color the meats and bones in the oven, then put them in a large marmite along with the trotters, the pork rind, the vegetables—except the green of the leek—and the aromatics, salt, and pepper. Cover with 8 quarts of water and leave to cook for 6 hours. Sieve and degrease completely.

To clarify, chop the lean beef finely. Chop also the green of the leeks. Mix with 6 lightly beaten egg whites. Put this mixture in a big enough, thick-bottomed marmite. Pour the warm stock on to the mix. Set on a medium fire and bring to a boil, whisking without stopping. Be careful that the mix does not stick to the bottom of the pan. Burnt gelée is lost. If, at this moment, the gelée does not seem to be setting, you can add a few leaves of gelatin dissolved in cold water.

Leave to cool. Add, as you feel, Madeira, Cognac, Alsace wine, Champagne . . . but do not to add the wine while the gelée is still hot, as it will lose its perfume.

GLOSSARY OF COOKING TERMS

Anglaise: Beat together one egg, a tablespoon of water, a tablespoon of olive oil, a pinch of salt, and a little pepper until it is a foam. Use as a batter for frying.

Bain-marie: Using two pans—the outer filled with water—to cook a dish in the inner. Used for scrambled eggs, béarnaise sauce, etc.

Bard: To wrap poultry or fish in, usually, fatty cuts of bacon or ham.

Bind: To thicken a sauce with cornstarch, an egg yolk, or cream.

Blanch: To cook briefly in boiling water.

Bouquet garni: A bundle of herbs—usually parsley, thyme, bay, and celery—wrapped in muslin and used for flavoring dishes. The bundle is removed from the pan or dish before serving.

Bouillon: The cooking liquid in which meats or vegetables have been cooked.

Braise: To cook using a minimum of liquid in a covered pan.

Chantilly: Cream that is whipped by a mixer, whisk, or fork until light and fluffy, and sweetened with sugar. Sometimes flavored with vanilla. Called Chantilly cream or *crème Chantilly*.

Clarify: To clear a jelly or a consommé by heating with cuts of lean beef, egg white, leeks, and aromatic herbs. Clarify also refers to when butter is melted down slowly to eliminate impurities and give it the quality of oil. The term can also mean to carefully separate an egg white from an egg yolk.

Cocotte: A cast-iron casserole cooking dish.

Concasse: Coarsely chopped.

Court bouillon: Literally a "short bouillon." Boiled with aromatics, usually used for cooking fish.

Deglaze: To wet the bottom of a pan or tray, after cooking, to make a jus.

Degrease: To take the fat off a sauce.

Dodine: Literally deboned—usually of poultry—so it can be stuffed and rolled.

Fines herbes: A herb combination of fresh parsley, chives, tarragon, and chervil.

Flambé: To baste with alcohol and set alight.

Fond: A concentrated court bouillon, destined for making sauces.

Fumet: A liquid fond, as opposed to a jelly.

Julienne: Batons of vegetables, truffles, and so on, of about two inches long and one-eighth of an inch wide.

Lardons: Little cubes of pork or bacon used to flavor casseroles.

Marmite: A large, lidded cooking dish, usually made of earthenware or metal.

Mirepoix: Carrots, shallots, onions, and so on, cut into small dice and used to season a reduction.

Mornay: A béchamel sauce made with Parmesan and gruyère.

Mousseline: Puree of meat, fish, or goose liver, to which whipped cream or beaten egg whites are added to lighten.

Pot au feu: Translated as "pot on the fire," it is a traditional beef and vegetable stew in France.

Reduce: To boil down a liquid in order to thicken and intensify its flavor.

Salmis: A stew made with game or duck.

Salpicon: One or more ingredients, diced or ground, and bound with a sauce.

Provençal tomatoes: Tomatoes that have been sliced in half, filled with chopped garlic, parsley, and bread crumbs, and baked.

Velouté: A cream sauce—literally, like velvet.

RECIPE FINDER